BLUES
GUITAR
RULES

Concepts and techniques for traditional and modern blues guitar

in the styles of
Robert Johnson
Albert King
Eric Clapton
Stevie Ray Vaughan
Robben Ford
Gary Moore
and many more

Impressum

All Rights reserved
Copyright © 1995 by
AMA Verlag GmbH
Postfach 1168
D-50301 Brühl
Germany

Coverdesign: Patrizia Obst, Cologne
Fotos: Uplegger, Berlin (S. 38, 51, 58, 61, 67, 85, 90, 104)
      Dieter Stork, Neuenkirchen-Seelscheid (S. 50, 59, 132)
      Klaus Erich Haun (S. 43)
      Fotex, Hamburg (S. 63)
      Virgin (S. 107)
      WEA, Köln (S. 87, 97, 101)
      TELDEC Rec., Hamburg (S. 65)
      Epic/CBS, Frankfurt (S. 92)
DTP: René Teichgraeber

ISBN 3-927190-64-0

Preface

Hello and welcome to "Blues Guitar Rules"! Rules for the blues? I guess this title could seem a bit paradoxical for some people, since the blues is, after all, the very epitome of feeling-oriented music. Aside from the fact that "feeling" just might be the single most important rule in this book, a closer look at the blues offers more than just a change of pace or an alternative to eight finger tapping. But what meaning could the blues have for a skinny white boy like myself?

As I was studying at GIT in Los Angeles in 1989/90 there were more or less regular concerts featuring guest artists every Thursday. One Thursday Albert Collins and band were advertised in the program. Now I must say, quite honestly, that I'd heard the name before, but that was about all I knew about Albert Collins. That this evening would be one of the most important events of my entire stay at GIT was something that didn't even occur to me until the first encore. The concert was pretty good, but as Mister Collins' playing was not exactly the apex of technical wizardry, it didn't really knock me out. Up to that point, I'd always associated the term blues more with people like Robben Ford, etc.. That all changed, however, with the last song of the evening as Albert Collins began to walk, through the audience (as he did every evening, as far as I know) with a ca. 200 meter long Guitar cord personally "bluesifying" every single listener in the hall. And although I had been standing somewhere where I was hoping he would miss me , I suddenly found myself face-to-face with the "Iceman". Being not much more than a foot away from him, I was pretty much trapped – escape was impossible. So I looked the persuasive bluesman right in his well worn face as he played right at me and shouted "C'mon skinny white boy, get the god damn blues!". I was transfixed, but Collins had already moved on to deliver the blues to the next soul.

Now this experience didn't quite affect me like the light in the church did blues brother Jake, but it gave me a kick that led me to a more "real" contact with the music and the meaning of the term blues. Obviously, this feeling was so strong and important for Mr. Collins that he didn't hesitate to preach the blues, even to a unknowing white kid.

A part of my research on blues and the influence that it's had on rock guitar can be found in my first book "Masters of Rock Guitar". As in the book that followed it, "Rock Guitar Secrets", I'd like to go in depth into the practica and theoretical concepts of blues guitar.

A look at the table of contents will show that I've covered all the important technical, rhythm and improvisational concepts; I hope that "Blues Guitar Rules" will serve you well as a comprehensive learning tool for blues guitar.

I've started with stage 1 – Easy Blues, in which I've described the development and basis of blues guitar. This part of the book is– on account of its simple but authentic sounding examples– particularly good for beginners..

Stage 2 – Blues and Rock Styles – goes off more in the rock direction and gives you, with authentic-sounding rhythmic figures and blues solos in the style of Clapton, Hendrix, Robben Ford, Stevie Ray Vaughan, Gary Moore and others, an insight into the concepts and licks of these guitarists.

The more I have to do with the subject, the clearer it is to me that the Blues is not only the feeling and groove basis for every style of rock and pop, but that you can use this fundamental musical form to explain just about every jazz and harmonic theory. I couldn't resist being pulled in this direction, "closet jazzer" that I am, so the result was stage 3 – Jazz Blues. In this section a number of concepts that come from jazz can be found, that can also be used in the context of a Strat and a turned up Marshall.

This brings me to the next point: the accompanying CD. On the CD you'll find a great number of examples and blues jam-tracks. To experience the optimal benefits of this book, you should work with both the book **and** the CD. Unfortunately written music is sometimes only half the truth. Particularly with the blues the ears have to be used in order to really understand the phrasing of the examples. The same goes, of course, for intensive listening to blues recordings, without which the much sought after blues feeling is unattainable.

Blues Guitar Rules? Rules for Blues Guitar... fortunately there's another way to look at this phrase. "To rule", as you may know, is also ghetto slang for to "reign", to be the best or coolest. That sense of the phrase expresses my basic feeling. So ...

At this point I'd like to thank a number of people that made my life and the writing of this book easier: Birgit Fischer, Olaf Krüger, Mark Skerra, Harald vo Falkenstein (Peavey) and Dieter Roesberg (Gitarre & Bass).

For the most diverse kinds of inspiration I'd like to thank Albert Collins, Stevie Ray Vaughan, Carl Schroeder, Steve Vai, Paulo Gilberto, Steve Lukather, Peter Paradise as well as all my guitar students.

Stay tuned, play hard, be real!

Peter Fischer

Table of Contents

Outline: The Study Plan

Stage 1 Easy Blues

Chapter	Theory	Practical Application
Chapter 1 Blues Basics, Part 1	- Harmony, rhythm and forms of the blues	- construction of the dominant and minor blues - shuffle rhythm, 12, 8, 16 + 24 bar forms for dominant and minor blues.
Chapter 2 Simple Blues Rhythm Patterns	- Single note riffs - powerchords and chord accompaniments for the dominant and minor blues	- riffs - chord voicings - ryhthm patterns - projects
Chapter 3 Turnarounds	- The Function and Structure of Turnarounds in the Blues Form - Bridging the gap: from rhythm guitar to solo playing	- single note riffs - interval riffs for tunarounds in dominant and minor blues - projects
Chapter 4 Easy Blues Lead Guitar	A - Musical material: minor and major pentatonic, blues scales B - Improvisational structures: AAB form, call and response C - Playing techniques: hammer-ons, pull-offs, sliding string bending, vibrato. D - Slide guitar: string action, types of slides, playing techniques, open tunings, phrasing E - Blues feeling: dirty intonation	- finger positions - exercises - example solos - projects
Chapter 5 Easy and Early Blues Styles	- introduction to the styles of **Robert Johnson, Muddy Waters, John Lee Hooker, B.B. King** and **Albert King**	- example solos - sound and playing tips - discography

Stage 2 Blues Rock Styles

Chapter	Theory	Practical Application
Chapter 6 Blues Basics, Part 2	– Modes in dominant and minor blues – scale combinations, arpeggios, the harmonic minor in minor blues – double time shuffle	– fingering positions – projects – example solos
Chapter 7 The Blues Rock of the 60's and 70's	– Introduction to the styles of **Jimi Hendrix**, **Eric Clapton** and **Duane Allmann**	– example solos – sound and playing tips – discography
Chapter 8 Texas Blues	– Introduction to the styles of **SRV** and **Billy Gibbons**	– example solos – sound and playing tips – discography
Chapter 9 Fusion Blues	– Introduction to the playing of **Larry Carlton** and **Robben Ford** – suspended chords – tension and resolution – arpeggio substitution	– example solos – sound and playing tips – chord voicings – chord progressions
Chapter 10 Modern Blues Rock	– Introduction to the style of **Gary More** and modern blues metal	– example solos – sound and playing tips – chord progressions – string skipping

Stage 3 Jazz Blues

Chapter	Theory	Practical Application
Chapter 11 The Dominant Jazz Blues	– Construction, note material and chord substitutions for the dominant jazz blues	– diminished seventh chords – II–V–I progressions in major and minor – altered dominant seventh chords – tritone substitution – modal interchange – chord progressions and voicings
Chapter 12 The Minor Jazz Blues	– Construction, note material and chord substitution for the minor jazz blues	– II–V–I progressions in minor and major – dominant seventh chords – altered dominant seventh chord – tritone substitution – major/minor relatives – chord progressions
Chapter 13 The Major Jazz Blues	– Construction, note material and chord substitutions for the major blues	– II–V–I progressions in major and minor – modal interchange – tritone substitution – chord progression
Chapter 14 Jazz Blues Comping	– 1–3–7 voicings – walking bass lines – chord scales – II–V–I patterns	– chord voicings and example choruses
Chapter 15 Jazz Blues Turnarounds	– Turnaround progressions for the dominant, minor and major jazz blues – note material for the above-mentioned turnarounds	– chord progressions – tritone substitution – walking bass lines – the common tone principle – diminished chords – chord melody – turnarounds – intros
Chapter 16 Jazz Blues Licks and Lines	– Licks for II–V–I progressions in major and minor – turnaround licks	– licks – fingering positions – projects
Chapter 17 Classic Blues Sounds		

CD Playlist Blues Guitar Rules

Index	chapter	title	
1	Simple rhythm guitar patterns	example	1 - 18
2	Turnarounds	example	11 - 31
3	Easy blues lead guitar	example	32 - 36
4	Easy and early blues styles	example	37 - 41
5	Blues basics part 2	example	42 + 43
6	Blues rock of the 60's and 70's	example	44 - 46
7	Texas blues	example	47 + 48
8	Fusion blues	example	49 + 50
9	Modern blues rock	example	51 + 52
10	Dominant jazz blues	example	53
11	Jazzblues comping	example	54 - 71
12	Jazzblues turnarounds	example	86 -103
13	Jazzblues licks and lines	example	104 - 125
14	Dominant blues forms	jamtrack	1
15	Minor blues forms	jamtrack	2
16	B.B. King style	jamtrack	3
17	Albert King style	jamtrack	4
18	Larry Carlton style	jamtrack	5
19	Robben Ford style	jamtrack	6
20	Gary Moore style	jamtrack	7
21	Modern metal style	jamtrack	8
22	Dominant jazz blues	jamtrack	9
23	Minor jazz blues	jamtrack	10
24	Major jazz blues	jamtrack	11

The CD was recorded between 12.28.92 and 01.03.93 at Hit'n'Run Studios, Lüdenscheid, Germany.

Peter Fischer: guitar and bass

Olaf Krüger: drum programing

Bodo Schulte: sound engineering and keyboards

Six tips for practicing

Before we get to the first chapter, here are a few ideas about effective studying and practicing that I feel have made guitar playing easier for me.

PRACTICING DAY AND NIGHT?

Do your practising at that time of day (or night) which is individually just the right time for you! For some, the morning is better, for others (me, for example) late at night. What's important is to find a healthy balance of discipline and the desire to play. If you've had a bad day and haven't practiced, it's not the end of the world. The best thing is to work with a daily practice program. It's also important to keep two days a week practice-free for things like jamming, in order to give your head time to assimilate and process what you've been practicing.

LEARNING IN LITTLE "CHUNKS"

It should be clear that, in principle, the study of the guitar (as well as every other instrument) is divided into two phases. One is the cognitive, meaning the mind - oriented learning process, for example the understanding and absorbing of a lick, a solo, a scale, or a particular technique. The other phase is the motoric learning process, the practical application, the actual playing and practicing until you've got what you've learned under your fingers.
These two approaches should be kept separate and practiced in completely different ways.
Modern research on learning has shown that an adult can concentrate on a particular subject for about two minutes. Pretty short, isn't it? So try to break up what you're learning into small pieces. You'll find that you'll get a lot further that way, and that it's easier to connect many little bits later on into a bigger piece than it is to swallow that big piece all at once. And believe me the smaller the pieces are, the faster and bigger the results will be. Try to really master the material before going on to the motoric phase. Here it's also important to try to avoid making the same mistake twice. If you're having trouble, maybe the chunks were too big.

Nothing hinders progress more than an overload.

Things are a bit different with the other phase. Once you've understood one of these "chunks" (for example, the first five notes of a scale) you can practice it as long as you wish, until you've attained the speed you want or until you drop from exhaustion. You should bear in mind that this means you can only play it better, and not that you understand it better. The actual cognitive learning process should only be a matter of two minutes at most and not more.

LONG AND SHORT TERM GOALS

Set yourself goals, and try to maintain them!!
Its important to distinguish between long and short-term goals. A long-term goal could be, for example, learning how to improvise fluently through difficult chord changes. This task can be divided up into work on scales, arpeggios, etc. These can be further broken down into individual positions, and so on. What's important is that you set these goals, no matter how modest they may be, formulating them in words or perhaps even writing them down, and that you try to attain them instead of just practicing aimlessly. Remember:

Every long journey begins with the first step!

PRACTICING MORE AND GETTING WORSE?

If you practice a lot you'll regularly get the feeling that you're getting worse instead of better. THIS IS NORMAL! This is a sign that your brain needs energy to assimilate the new material. Don't get uptight. As soon as your head is free again, this feeling will disappear. You'll find that your old licks, plus the new ones, will work again when this process is completed.

DO IT YOURSELF!

This is a "do it yourself" book.
Like guitar lessons, or other guitar books, this book can merely give you theoretical and technical tips and suggestions. This book will not teach you how to play the guitar! You have to do that yourself. There's no way around it. You have to take the guitar in your hands, play it and get better. All my book can do is to make the going a bit easier.

MUSIC IS FUN!

This is the most important realization I've come to: **music is fun**.
Even if you've got great ambitions as a guitarist or see the guitar as your life's focal point, have fun with it and try to experience the music as something beautiful without weighing it down with unnecessary seriousness.
If you still find yourself on a downer, imagine, from this moment on, **never** being able to play again ... Feel better now?

The Story of the Blues
– How the Blues came to be

"Tryin' to get away from a pain you can't live with and a woman you can't live without." Its impossible to determine the beginning of an era in music or art in terms of a fixed day, and the blues is no exception, particularily as this music is the result of culturally different populations crashing into contact with one another. The history of the blues began on different continents during the 17th century, a time at which music theory had become pretty well-developed in Europe in classical music. The trading of black African slaves and their shipment to the New World, America, began around the same time. Between 1620 and 1850 approximately half a million blacks were brought from West Africa to New Orleans and other cities where they were transported further up the Mississippi to work on the plantations along the river. They brought thousand year-old rhythms with them, ritual in origin and totally untheoretical. Most of the slaves were deprived of any rights and were allowed nothing more than to sing while working in the fields. It was in these fields that a form called "call and response" developed, in which the foreman would call out a phrase and the workers would answer. Often such singing would carry double meanings and hidden references, allowing them to vent their feelings about their poor living conditions. The only joy in their lives were parties on Saturday night or church services which served a similar function.

The end of the civil war in 1865 brought an official end to slavery, but living conditions didn't improve much for most southern blacks, and many moved up north. The era of gospel and spitituals came to a high point during this period. The most popular instruments of the time were banjo, fiddle and toward the end of the century the guitar became increasingly popular as well. The first music played by blacks to become popular in America was ragtime, above all the music of **Scott Joplin** ("The Entertainer") around the turn of the century. Another important name during these times was **W.C. Handy**, a roaming bandleader who in 1914 published the "St. Louis Blues" using the term "blues" for the first time in a song title.

From around the turn of the century into the 1920's and 30's a number of different country blues styles developed. Although they all evolved more-or-less simultaneously these regional variations remained independent and different from one another. One area was the Mississippi Delta where artists such as **Charlie Patton, Son House** and **Robert Johnson** played. Another area was Dallas, Texas, where musicians like **Leadbelly, Blind Lemon Jefferson** and **Tampa Red** could be heard. A third "stream" of black music was the "classic blues" which was dominated by singers such as **Bessie Smith**, who combined bluesy vocals with traditional folk songs and ballads. The tremendous economic problems of the times also affected many of the already footloose blues musicians, who moved on to Chicago, seeking better fortunes. In the "windy city" during the 20's, jazz was flourishing with musicians such as trumpeter **Louis Armstrong.**

Alongside the blues of **Big Bill Broonzy** and **Lonnie Johnson**, Jazz and Swing developed at this time as well with bands of increasing size led by the likes of **Duke Ellington, Benny Goodman** and **Count Basie** and singers such as **Ella Fitzgerald**. At the end of the 30's a guitarist by the name of **Charlie Christian** played with the **Benny Goodman** band who is credited with having been the first "electrified" guitarist, giving the guitar an equal place alongside the other jazz instruments. The spread of radios and jukeboxes brought an explosion of popularity to blues music. Chicago remained a musical center with guitarists such as **Muddy Waters, Elmore James** and **Howling' Wolf** and the term "Chicago blues" was coined. The blues in Texas was formed and influenced by **T-Bone Walker**, and at the same time **John Lee Hooker** was making a sensation in Detroit. Thus the blues occupied a permanent place in the musical culture of postwar America and influenced the later development of rock music, laying the foundations for modern popular music.

Stage 1

Easy Blues

The Blues Made Simple

Chapter 1
Blues basics, part I

I think it is important, before we begin to work on the "official" blues licks and grooves, that we look first at the main components of blues.

Fortunately, in this style of music things are pretty straightforward, so this won't be difficult. There are numbers of factors that are crucial to the stylistic formation of any kind of music, whether blues, rock, trash metal, jazz or folk music.

a) Harmony (chords used and how they are connected)
b) Melody (we'll be giving this topic a thorough treatment in the coming chapter on solo guitar)
c) Rhythm
d) Form of the song

Because of its historical sources and its being a mixture of different musical cultures the blues presents a unique fusion of those different influences.

The Blues Harmony

The harmonic aspects of blues are, so to speak, the european part of this music style. In early blues such as swing and dixieland tunes the chord progressions are practically identical to those which can be found in european folk and pop music (that's a shock, eh?). As this is a blues book and not a collection of folk songs, I won't spend much time on this.

Here is a C major scale.

You can build a chord on each step of the scale. In the language of music theory this is called harmonization. This process yields the following chords. Using the chords on the 1st, 4th and 5th step of the scale one can accompany almost every folk or pop song.

These three chords have a name: the chord on the first step is called the **tonic** (T), representing the basic key of the song. The chord built on the 4th step is called the **subdominant** (SD), it moves, soundwise, away from the tonic. The chord built of the 5th step is called the **dominant** and moves back towards the tonic. This effect is intensified if you add an extra note (f) making the G major chord into a G^7 chord (as in the above). Hence the other term for this chord: the dominant seventh chord.

Now let's get back to the blues. Basically the blues can be divided harmonically into two groups: dominant and minor. In the area of jazz another sort of blues has cropped up: the major blues. As it is an interesting variation of normal jazz blues form, I'll be discussing it later on in detail.

The Dominant Blues

Until about 1920 the blues form (more on this term in a moment) looked, more or less, like this:

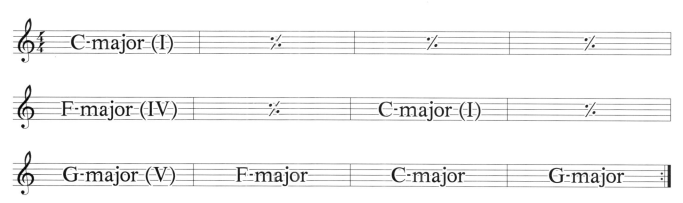

So now we come to something that still makes hard-core classic freaks tear out their hair: one changes all three chords to dominant seventh chords. Whose idea it was is something no one knows anymore. The sound effect is pretty crass. The tensions that the dominant seventh chords have are no longer neatly resolved to a major or minor tonic (as is usual in classical music) but just sit there hanging around with the other dominant 7th chords.

Here's what it looks like:

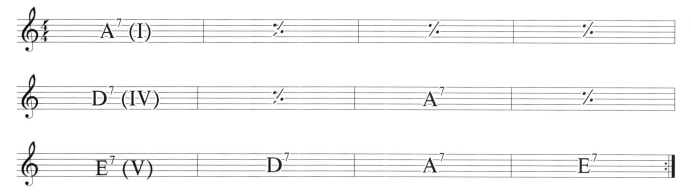

This 12 bar form is what one generally means by blues or blues form in today's musical language.

The Minor Blues

To get from the dominant blues over to the minor blues is quite simple: all dominant chords are turned into minors.

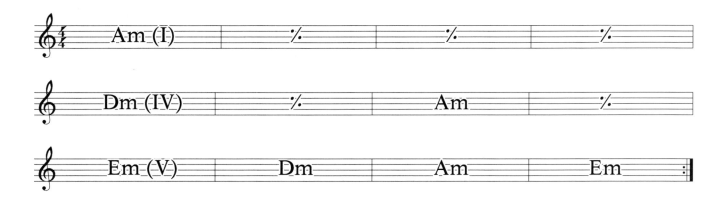

This form has been changed too, however, and often the chord built on the 5th step is changed to a dominant 7th to give it more tension:

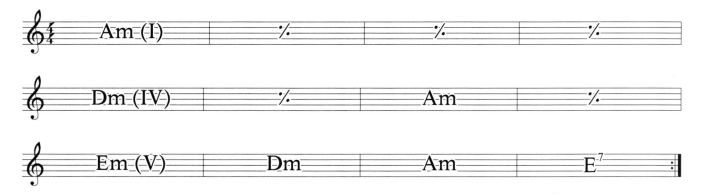

This form is the second standard blues form. To me it sounds even "bluesier" than the dominant blues.

By the way, if you play the above forms with power chords, both will be the same because of the missing third in the power chord.

The Rhythm of the Blues

Another very important element of the blues "recipe" is, of course, the shuffle rhythm, imported with the African slaves. This is a rolling rhythm that keeps the feet tapping. But what is a shuffle, really? In order to understand this we will first have to bring two new words into the picture: binary and ternary rhythms.

Next page you see a "rhythm pyramid" in which we've categorized each note value as binary or ternary divisions.

The Rhythm Pyramid

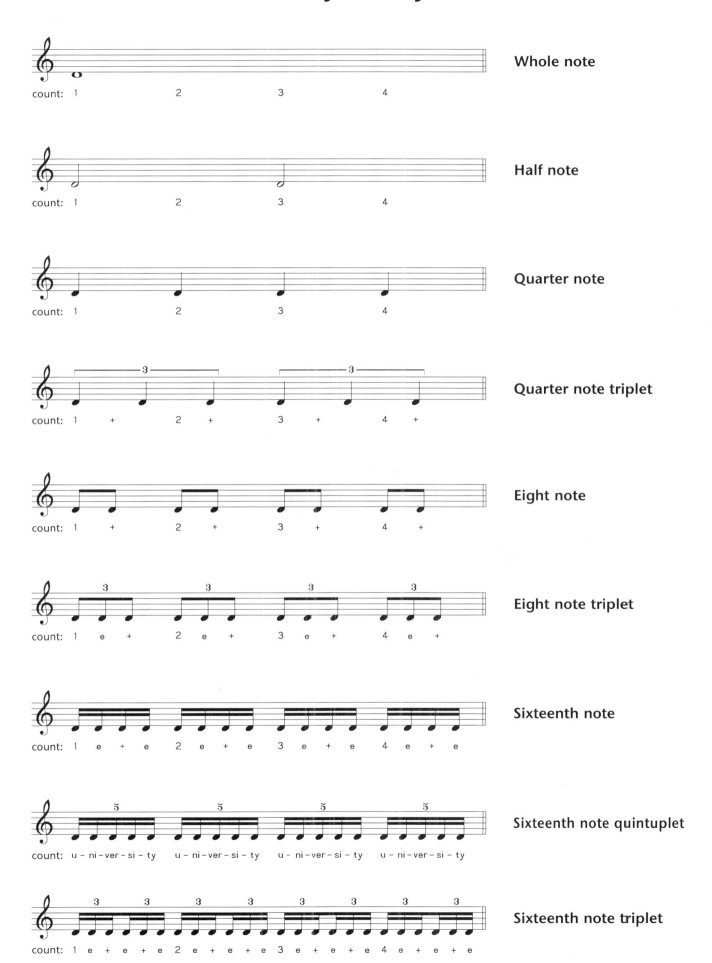

For the blues, the lines with the eighth notes and the eighth note triplets are most important. Eighth notes are the binary subdivision of quarter notes; they are counted like this:

The ternary subdivision of the quarter notes, the eighth note triplets, are counted like this:

There are two ways to describe the shuffle rhythm:
1. the middle note of the triplet is left out;

2. the second note of the triplet is "tied" to the first.

Both come out to one and the same thing, the first sounds a bit staccato, the second has a bit more "swing".

To simplify matters, this ryhthm is usually notated as normal eighth notes, but at the beginning of the song it is written:

This shuffle rhythm is found in almost every blues in contrast to the "straight" or "smooth" eighth notes in Rock'n'Roll songs (e.g. in Chuck Berry songs).

Now that we understand the harmonic and rhythmic aspects, we can turn our attention to the next important element of blues: the form.

The Forms of Blues

As the blues is basically a type of folk music, musicians in different regions tended to have a common understanding of blues feeling, but often used different song forms. Thus the so-called blues forms vary in length and chord structure. Here are a few blues forms; all of them are used today and have their own qualities (all examples in A) :

Blues Forms for the Dominant Blues

The standard 12 bar blues.

Here is the classic 12 bar blues that's most commonly.

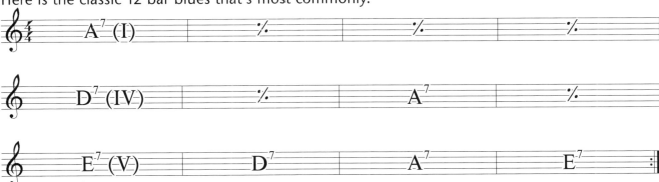

The standard 12 bar blues with a "quick change".

Note, in this form, the second and last two measures. The chord change in the second measure to the IV chord is refered to as a "quick change".

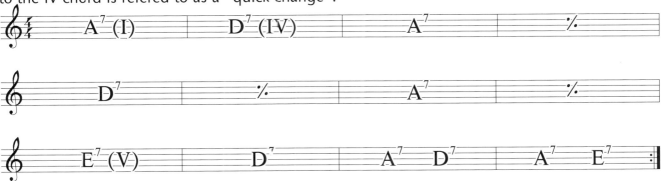

The 12 bar "King Bee" blues.

This variation sounds a little bit more "cheerful" in the middle than the other forms, and is already a step in the direction of jazz blues (see stage III p. 113).

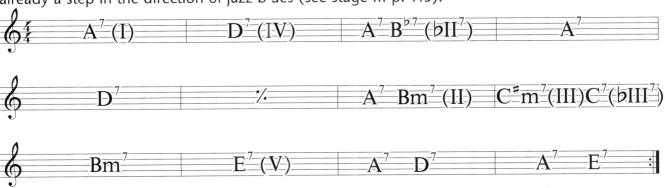

The 24 bar blues.

This blues form has an identical chord progression as the first one, but every chord is now held out twice as long.

The 8 bar blues form # 1.

Here is a shorter version of the 8 bar blues, based on the Freddie King Song "Key to the Highway".

The 8 bar blues form # 2.

This is a form that is often used as a verse in blues songs.

The 8 bar blues form # 3.

This scheme sounds a bit jazzier.

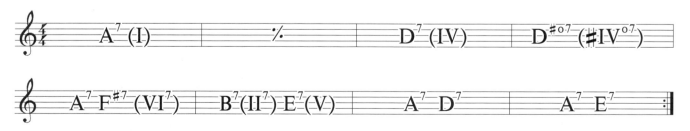

The 16 bar form # 1.

In the 16 bar form, the standard form is somewhat "stretched out".

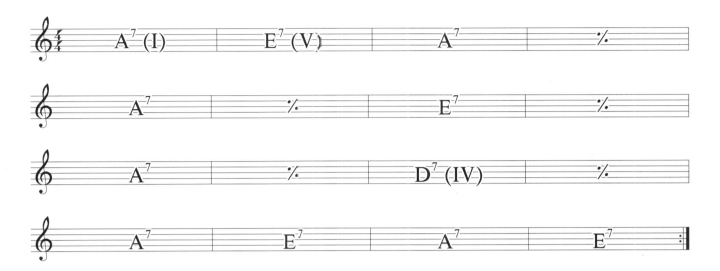

The 16 bar form # 2.

This form is often used as a middle section or bridge.

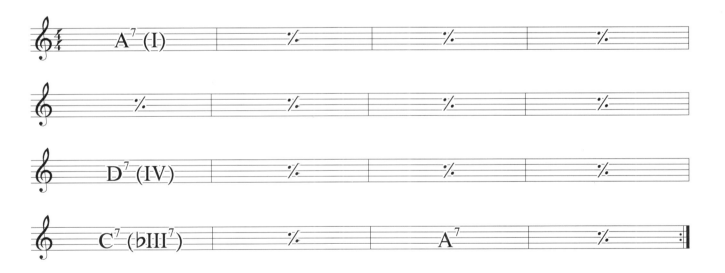

 All the blues forms can be heard on the CD, put together as Jamtrack 1. In order to help you differentiate various long forms I've given them different arrangements.

Blues Forms for the Minor Blues

As with the dominant blues you can also play around with it and change its form. Minor blues in 8 bar or 16 bar form are pretty rarely encountered in " real life".

The standard 12 bar minor blues form # 1.
This form is the starting point for the following variations.

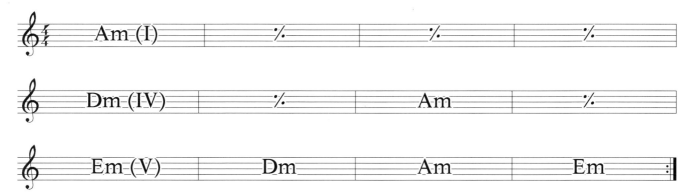

The standard 12 bar minor blues form # 2.
To make a stronger pull back to the tonic, one can turn the minor chord built on the fifth step into a dominant 7th chord.

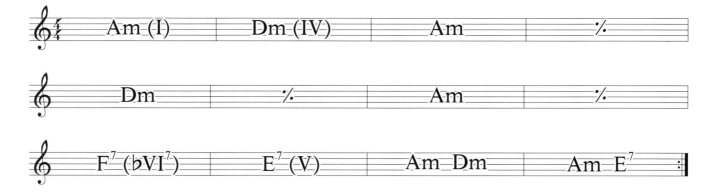

The standard 12 bar minor blues with "quick change".
Beside the quick change, you'll find a new chord in the 7th measure.

The standard 12 bar minor blues form # 3.

This form also sounds a bit jazzier because of the minor 7♭5 chord in the 9th measure.

Am (I)	Dm (IV)	Am	⅍
Dm	⅍	Am	⅍
Bm⁷♭⁵ (II)	E⁷ (V)	Am	E⁷

The 24 bar blues in minor.

Hits like Prince's "Kiss" show that the blues even has a place in modern pop music.

Am⁷ (I)	⅍	⅍	⅍	⅍	⅍	⅍	⅍
D⁷ (IV)	⅍	⅍	⅍	Am⁷	⅍	⅍	⅍
E⁷ (V)	⅍	D⁷	⅍	E⁷	⅍	E⁷	-

Project:

Listen to as many blues records as you can and try to recognize the above mentioned forms.

⚠ As with the dominant blues before, you can hear all of the forementioned minor blues forms together under "Jamtrack 2".

Chapter 2
Simple Blues Rhythm Patterns

So, enough talk! Now we come to a few simple–but–very–cool rhythm patterns that can be found (with minor variations) in hundreds of blues tunes. Off we go with:

Single Note Riffs

These first blues accompaniments are riffs, mostly playable in unison with the bass. They are made up of single notes and are not only quite simple to play but sound very authentic. All the following examples are written out in the key of A. To play them through the entire blues form, you only need to slide the fingerings around, with the tonic note finger sliding to the basic note of the respective chord in the form. In other words, the same riff for the IV chord (the subdominant) either one string over or 5 frets higher on the same strings. To get the riff on the V chord (dominant) you play either one string over and two frets higher, or on the same string seven frets higher. How you choose to do it is up to you. Try out the different possibilities. Depending on the fingering of the riff, one or the other will work better for you.

Here's an example:

Example
»1«
CD-INDEX 1

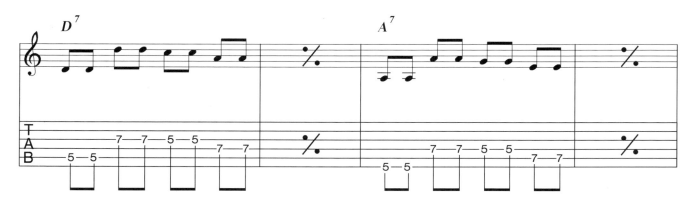

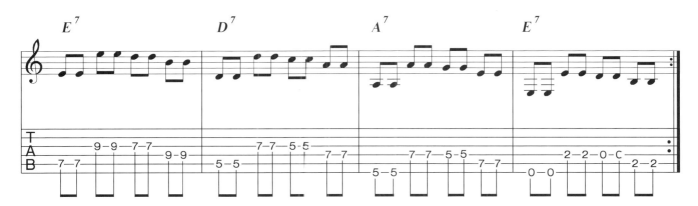

Try to play riffs that involve open strings with all notes fretted as well.
By the way, all the following patterns are to be played with a shuffle feel.

Example »2-5«  CD-INDEX 1

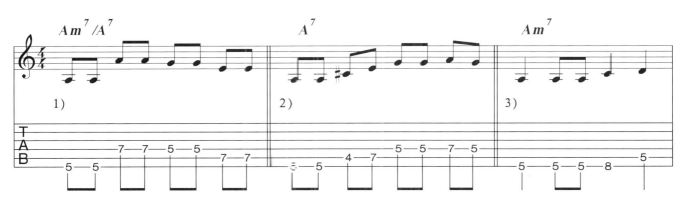

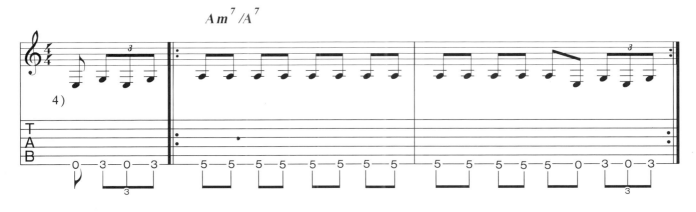

Powerchord accompaniments

After these single note riffs, we now come to a few variatons of some very well-known and often-played ways of playing a blues accompaniment. They are particularly well for "rock-ish" blues grooves. Except for the last one. These patterns sound the best when you mute the strings with the ball of the right hand.

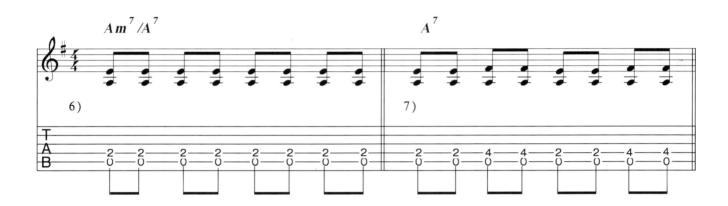

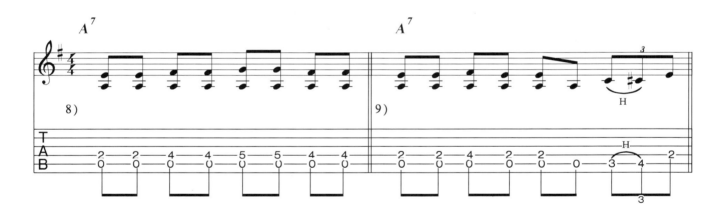

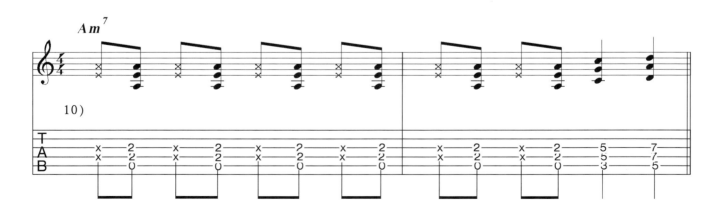

Chord accompaniments

The following accompaniments are more chord oriented. This first variation here is one that I call the "campfire" blues accompaniment, as it is made up of simple, open chords and is easy to play.

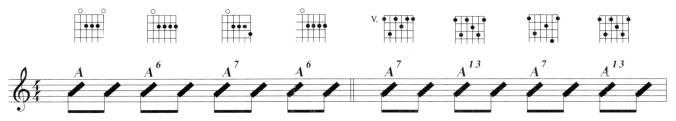

Example 11 is, on account of the open strings used in it, excellent for acoustic guitar. If you want to play the riff correctly over the other chords in the blues pattern, the fingerings have to be changed a bit.

Example »11« CD-INDEX 1

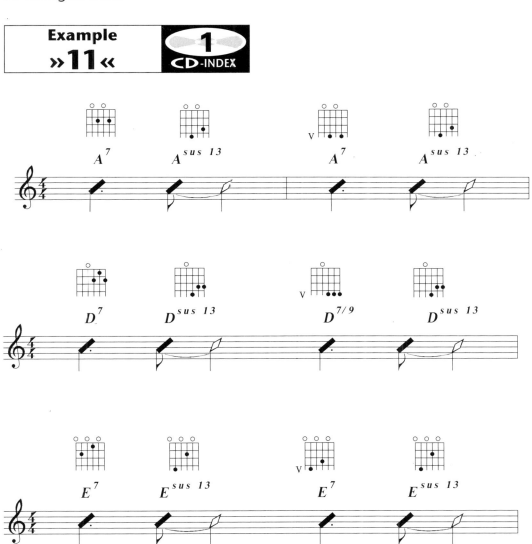

Here are a few good sounding dominant seventh chord voicings.
Although some of them are dom 9 or dom 13 chords, you can use them interchangeably. They sound a little more colorful than regular dominant 7th chords. To play them in a different key, simply slide the chord up or down the neck until the encircled tonic note sits on the proper place on the neck.

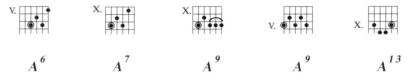

Play them with the following rhythm.

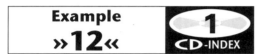

Project:

Play through the complete blues form using each one of these voicings. This will help you get to know the color of the different types of chords.

Next, try to use the different voicings like building blocks, switching and rearranging them without changing the set rhythm.

The next rhythm is easier than the preceding one, but "sliding into" the chord gives things a slightly jazzier touch. Try this out with all the chord voicings. By the way, you can just as easily slide into a chord from above as from below.

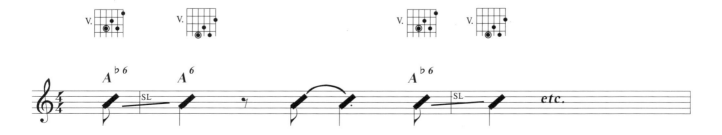

The two following patterns have a similar flair.

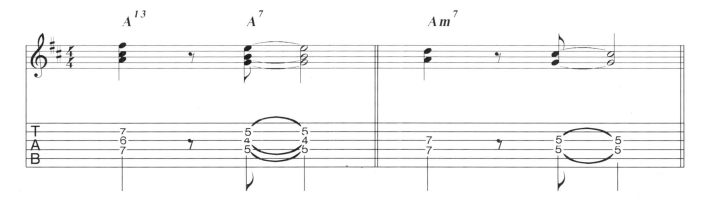

Like example 15, this is a "comping" (jazz slang for accompaniment) pattern for minor blues.

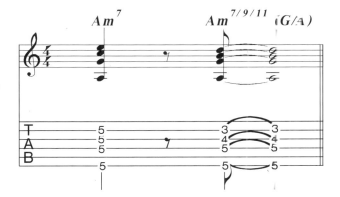

Project:

Try playing the above mentioned patterns on other string pairs as those notated.

Combine the different patterns with one another.

Record the blues form using different comping patterns and then try playing a different pattern over that line a second rhythm guitar, so to speak.

If you play the above mentioned rhythms with a "straight ahead" beat (without the shuffle feeling) you'll get a real good "instant rock'n'roll" accompaniment.

If the change to the IV chord comes too abruptly for your taste, you can lead into it with the following riffs. That is, in the 3rd measure, instead of the normal pattern, try:

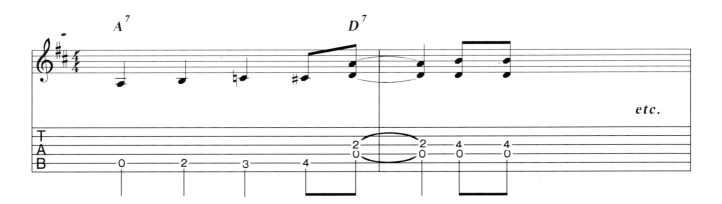

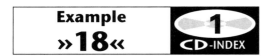

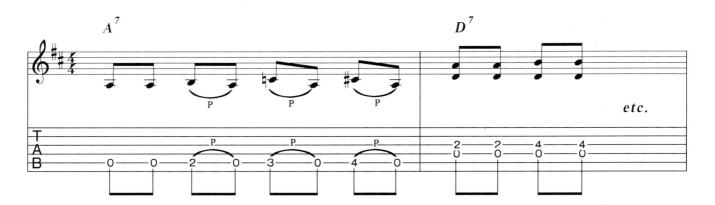

Chapter 3
The Turnaround

An important part of hip blues guitar playing, is knowing current and authentic melodic phrases and turns. A good place to begin is the turnaround. The what ???

The turnaround means the last two measures in the blues form.

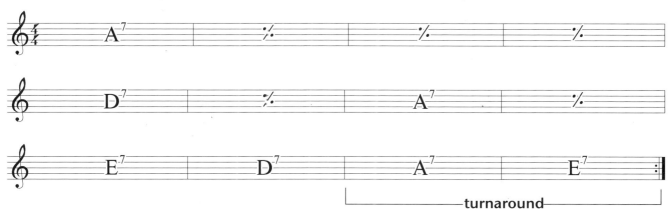

These two measures could also look like this.

In a minor blues, the turnaround looks like this

or like this

A turnaround means exactly what it says: it is a part of a musical form that turns around, or brings back to the beginning of the form.

The turnaround does not only sound good, of course, in the context of the choruses themselves, but also makes an excellent introduction for the song. Starting right in with the form never sounds quite as exciting as leading into your "statement" with an interesting phrase. So you can use all of the following phrases and licks as intros or as turnarounds in the form during the song.

The turnaround is also the part of the tune where the rhythm section gets to show what it can do harmonically. This can become quite involved, especially in the area of jazz, and can sometimes be pretty challenging for the ear (see and listen to chapter XV). In this chapter, however, instead of dealing with the harmonic possibilities offered by the turnaround, we'll restrict ourselves, first, to a few standard licks over the previously mentioned standard blues turnaround.

Bridging the gap: from rhythm guitar to solo playing

As we've been mostly concerned with rhythm guitar playing until now, playing blues phrases over the tunraround will be our initial crossing over fom rhythm to solo guitar playing. So ... in the part of the blues form where you played the turnaround – the last two measures – you will now be playing a turnaround lick. These licks also sound good in blues solos (see chapter IV); when played at the right point they demonstrate a real command and understanding of the form ("this guy knows what he's doing!").

Turnarounds in Dominant Blues

So ... enough talk! Here are a few hip turnarounds/intros:
The first four turnarounds sound especially good with comping patterns 6 – 9 from chapter 2
Turnaround 3 is more or less a combination of 1 and 2.

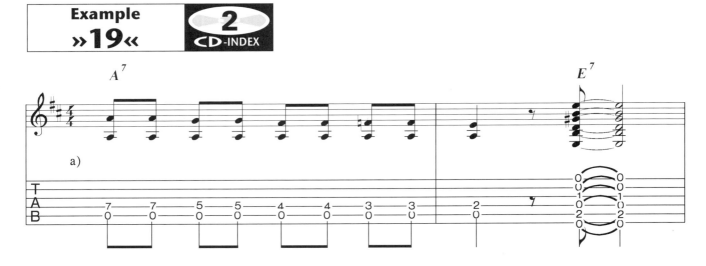

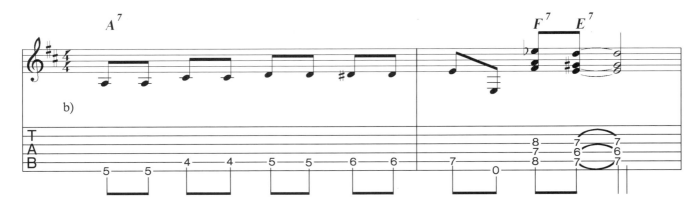

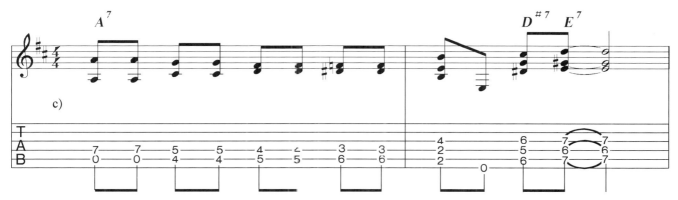

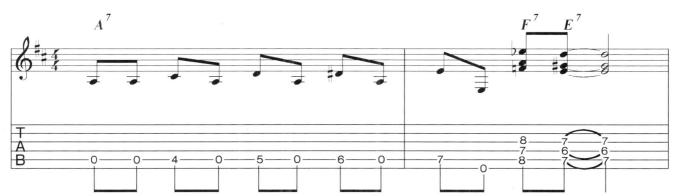

This turnaround only involves the last measure of the form.

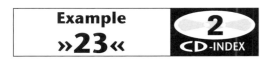

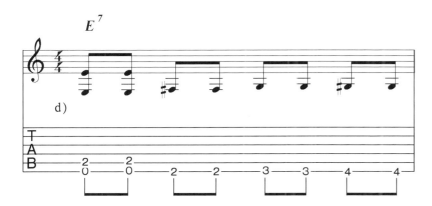

The next five phrases are variations on the concept of playing the turnaround with sixths. Try adding a little vibrato here.

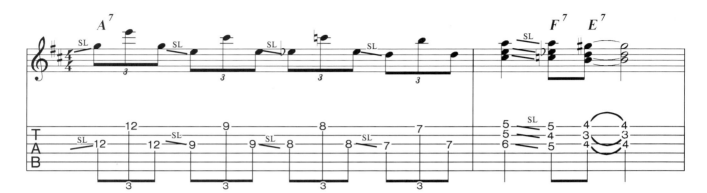

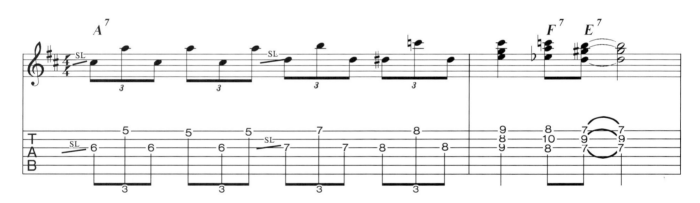

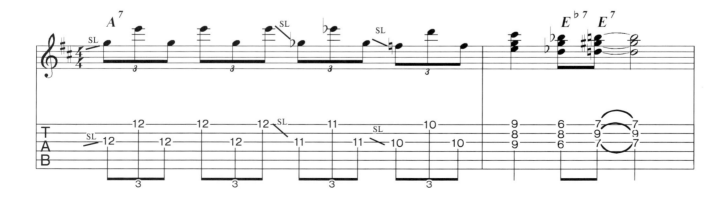

Example »27«

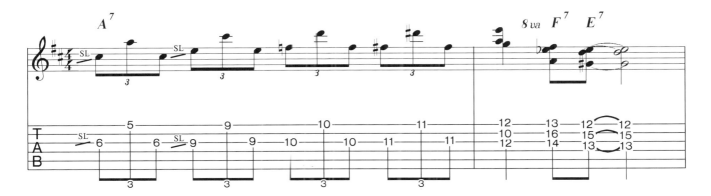

Example »28«

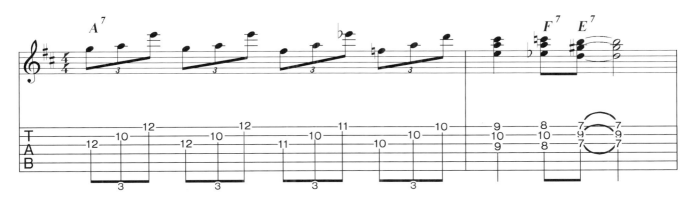

Example »29«

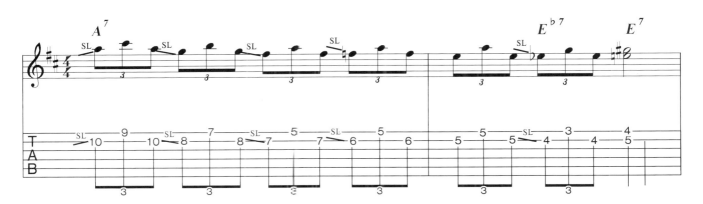

This is a bit more difficult.

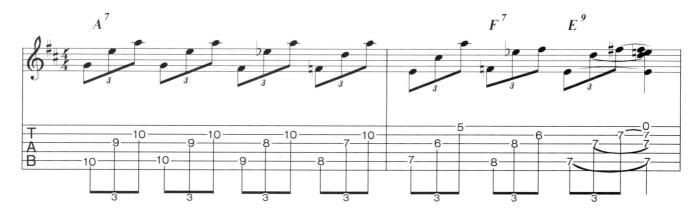

Turnarounds in Minor

There are far fewer turnaround "cliches" in minor blues than in dominant blues. Most of the chord progressions used here come from the minor jazz–blues (see chapter V). Here is a minor turnaround that comes more from rock.

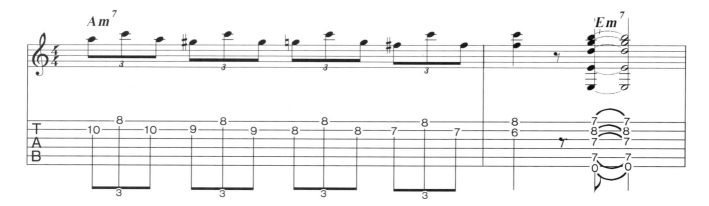

Project:

The right combinations makes it happen: combine the various rhythm guitar ideas from chapter III and the different forms from chapter II with the turnarounds.

Hey, you can play the blues in keys other than A!! (Just dropping a subtle hint).

Play the above mentioned turnarounds in other octaves and on other pairs of strings as well. Do it!

So ... in the next chapter we'll be looking at solo licks and ideas for the first ten measures of the blues form

Chapter 4
Easy Blues Lead Guitar

Welcome to lead guitar land!

As the chapter heading suggests, we are now going to get into some of the simple concepts of blues solo guitar. To approach this enormous area step-by-step, I've divided this chapter up into four areas each of which is an important element of improvising over the blues form: note material, solo construction, playing techniques and blues "feeling".

The Note Material, Part 1

For those who perhaps might not yet know what I mean by the term "note material", here's a short explanation: note material means the different possible note formations (scales, arpeggios, etc.) that can be used to improvise over a chord or chord progression.

The minor pentatonic

The minor pentatonic is the first in a series of scales that can be used to improvise in the blues and in other styles as well. With it you can produce quite a number of authentic blues sounds. The prefix "penta" comes from Greek and means "five". The pentatonic is a scale with five notes. The simplest explanation that I know of this scale is that, in comparison to the major or minor scales it contains no half steps which makes it very easy to play.

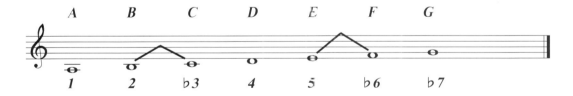

Here is a fingering position for the minor pentatonic. The encircled notes are the tonic notes.

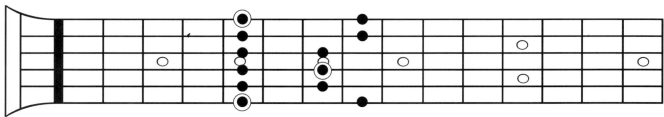

A-Moll-Pentatonik

Project:

Record a few minutes worth of "blues form" in A on tape (dominant as well as minor). Now play the A minor pentatonic over it.

Try, as you're jamming, to resolve your ideas to the tones (tonic, third, fifth, seventh) of the chord on which you're playing.

Over D⁷ play D minor pentatonic and over E⁷ the E minor pentatonic.

The Blues Scale

For my taste, the minor pentatonic sounds a little too smooth. It doesn't have any edges and no tension at all. This changes immediately if we add one note: the ♭5 or diminished fifth. The b5 is the chromatic note between the fourth and the fifth. This note removes the smoothness from the pentatonic and gives it more blues feeling.

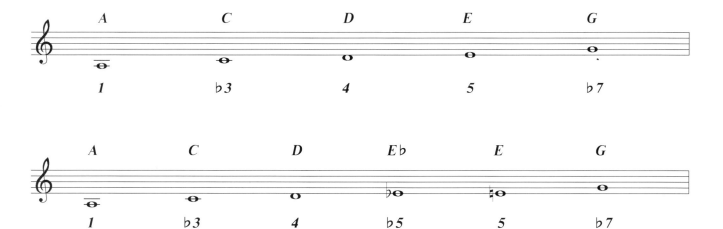

This note is generally referred to as the "blue note", although there are a few other notes that help to make the blues so "blue"; but we'll come to those later on. The ♭5 is absolutely the most dissonant, tension filled interval there is. Properly used, it can give your playing a lot of color in other styles as well.

Here is a fingering for the blues scale.

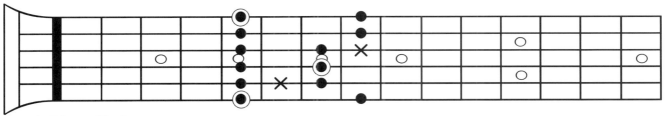

A-Blues-Skala

In order to make it more visible, I've marked the blue note with an X. As you can see, the only difference between the blues scale and the minor pentatonic is the blue note.

Project:

Repeat the previous project with the blues scale.

While improvising try to concentrate on playing the b5 in order to really feel its tonal color and dissonance.

Big Bill Broonzy

Solo Construction

At this point your solo improvisatons might not yet sound quite like those on your favorite records. This could be because you don't yet know how to construct, how to build up a solo. You've probably also wondered why I haven't given you any pentatonic or blues licks. There's a reason for this; in order to get a good feeling for the construction and dramatic building of a solo, I find that licks, at least at the beginning, get in the way. Later, of course, you can use licks quite effectively as fills, endings or turnarounds.

The "A-A-B" Form

In the beginnings of the blues, a certain form developed and established itself in sung verses and solos: the A-A-B form. Here is a sample lyric which should make this form clearer.

I was standing at the window tears running down my cheek

Standing at the window big tears running my cheek

I could see the woman I'm loving, stopping every man she meets

Example »32« | **3 CD-INDEX**

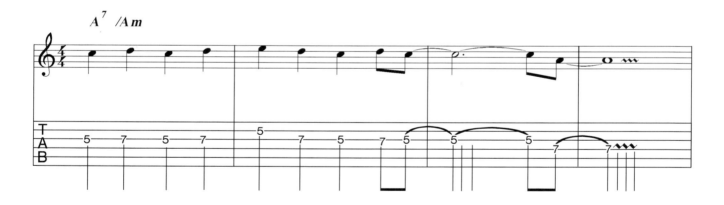

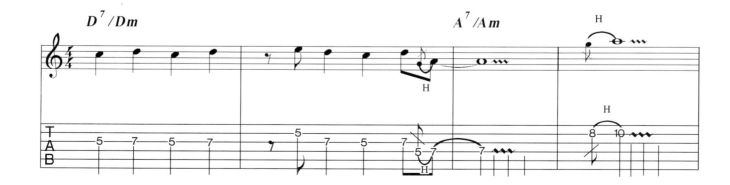

This solo can be "blocked out" into the following diagram.

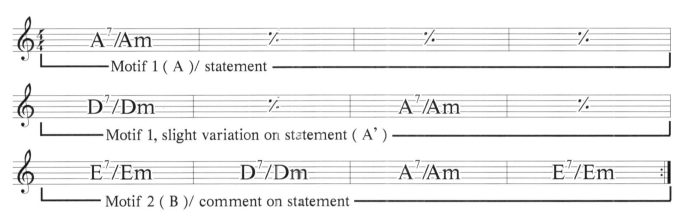

In measures 1 – 4 I play a simple motif (a musical idea or phrase). This is my "statement", comparable to the first line of the above mentioned blues lyric.

In measures 5 – 8 I repeat this motif, but with a somewhat different rhythm and ending. In measures 9 and 10 I make an answer to the two statements with a final motif.

Then I leave the last two measures pretty much empty in order to let the turnaround "do its job". Many people refer to this form as "call and response". It is a simple but effective way to structure a solo.

This solo might not yet be an authentic sounding blues solo, but it does, however, have the construction of a blues solo, similar to those which can be heard on many records (This does not mean, of course, that all blues solos have this structure).

As you can see, this solo has a good number of pretty empty spots which you can choose to fill out with licks and lines (longer melody lines) to give the solo more drive and flow.

Now it's up to you to develop and refine this raw material. To do this you can use:

    a) authentic playing techniques (string bending, vibrato, etc.);
    b) more "cool" notes (scales, arpeggios, etc.);
    c) fills, licks and lines;
    d) feeling.

Playing Techniques

Hammer-ons and pull-offs.

The alternative to "normal" playing technique in which every note is picked is legato technique. With this technique, as many notes as possible are sounded by means of hammer-ons and pull-offs instead of being produced by strokes from the right hand.

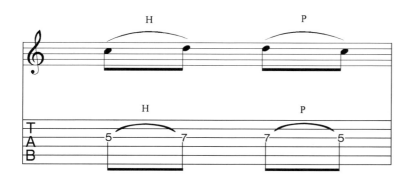

H = hammer-on

P = pull-off

Basically, anything that can be played with the right hand can also be played using legato technique only; the resulting sound is softer and more fluid.

By the way, if you're interested in excercises for perfecting this technique check out my book "Total Guitar Technique".

Slides

A simple but always good sounding technique for the electric guitar is the use of slides. Instead of directly playing the note, you can also slide into it from above or below.

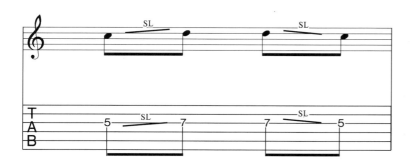

SL = slide

String Bending

If there is one single technique that is typical of the electric guitar, it's string bending.

Starting notes and target notes.

The important thing when bending notes is to bend cleanly to the right pitch. Bending too sharp or too flat sounds, to be honest, downright awful. That means that you should be completely aware of which tone you're trying to reach (target note).

First fret the note to which you want to bend, then finger two frets below it (starting note) and bend up to your target note. This is called a wholetone bend. The bent note should be as near as possible to the pitch of the first fretted note.

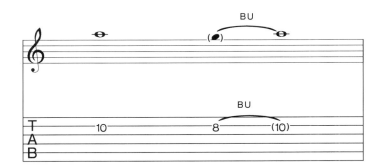

BU = Bend up

Now try reaching the same target note using different "starting" notes (halftone = 1 fret below, 1 1/2 tone = 3 frets below and two whole tones = 4 frets below). Although some bending is pretty hard on your "chops" it will bring a great deal of variety into your playing. Stevie Ray Vaughan, Albert King (among others) are evidence of the tremendous expressive potential that extreme bending can bring to your playing.

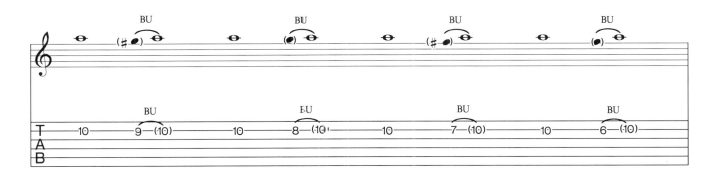

This exercise should be played on all strings, with all fingers and in all positions (as every string feels pretty different in different parts of the fingerboard). Is a different sound produced by using various fingers to bend notes? I'd say so ... This is, by the way, an extremely important aspect of playing blues solos.

The idea is not necessarily playing the most ornate or technically amazing licks. More important is playing simple phrases and ideas, repeating them and using variations in phrasing. In such a way that the ideas always sound new.

By the way: bending is much easier if the finger making the bend is supported by the fingers behind it (impossible, of course, when bending with the index finger). With the index finger you should, on the lower four strings, only bend in a downward direction. It also helps to save energy if you place your thumb over the top of the guitar neck, using it to counter the pressure from the bending finger. This basically turns the whole bending process into a contraction of the hand muscles.

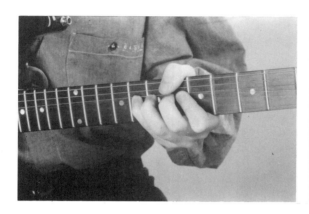 

right   wrong

One problem that often crops up with bending and vibrato is unwanted noise from the strings behind the hand. For this reason I usually position my hand like this while bending:

As my ring finger – supported by my middle finger – bends the string, my index finger mutes the other ones.

String Bending and Pentatonic

The following table shows how to effectively apply different-sized bends within the pentatonic scale.

STARTING NOTE	TARGET NOTE	EFFECT
A	1 whole step - B	extends the pentatonic scale; produced interval: 9, adds color
A	minor third - C	great intensity (Lukather)
C	1 whole step - D	standard rock bending
C	minor third - Eb	great intensity
C	major third - E	extreme intensity
D	half step - Eb	blue note; adds color
D	whole step - E	standard rock bending
E	whole step - F#	extends the pentatonic scale; produced interval (13), adds color in blues
E	minor third - G	high intensity
G	whole step - A	standard rock bending
G	major third - B	extends the pentatonic scale; produced interval (9), adds color

Project:

Think up a lick for each one of the above mentioned bends.

How do other guitarists play these bends? The answer can be heard on literally every rock or blues record.

Try learning the bending licks from your favorite records. At first this is a lot of sweat and hard work, but hey, remember that this used to be the only way to learn to play the electric guitar ... and a little bit of ear training now and then never hurts – so just do it!

Smear or Small Bend

For blues there is a particularly important bending technique called the smear or small bend. Here the note is only slightly bent about a quarter tone.

There are a few good notes for this to be found in the minor pentatonic. The most obvious one is the minor third (the C, for example, in A minor pentatonic). If you bend this note a quarter tone, the result is what I call the "blues third". This "sour" note between C and C♯ is just what you need to give your playing that authentic sound. This is another " blue note " like the ♭5. Here is the blues scale with the blues third added:

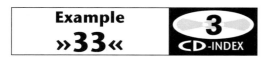

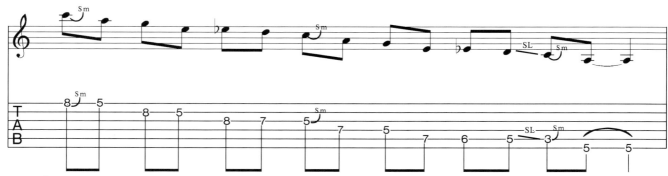

 Attention! The blues third sounds good only over the I and the V chord (e.g. in A over the A⁷ and E⁷), not over the IV chord.

Project:

How would this work with the other notes in the blues scale? How "blue" would they sound with a quarter tone bend? It's a question of your own personal taste.

Release Bend

The release bend sounds as though one is bending downwards. The trick to it is: before you hit the string bend up lightning fast and then, after the sounding of the string, release it, letting it come down slowly (or quickly, or however you feel it).

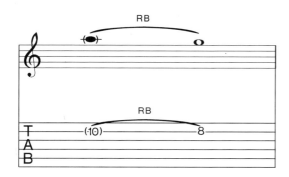

RB = release bend

Vibrato

Another very important playing technique which is related to bending is vibrato. The sort of vibrato most used in blues is the type that is a combination (similar to string bending) of a wrist and forearm motion. This movement is almost as if you were turning a key in a lock. The difference is that after the bending, the note immediately returns to the starting note. Here are a few ideas to keep in mind:

- After the bend, come right back exactly to the starting note or the vibrating note won't sound right.

- Practice your vibrato with a metronome. If you vibrate in time with the beat, your note will be integrated much better into the music as if you simply wobble around over the meter.

- Start with quarter notes, then try eighth notes, eighth note triplets and then sixteenth notes.

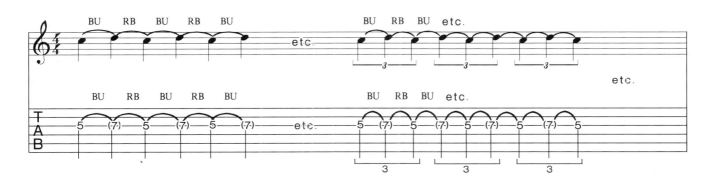

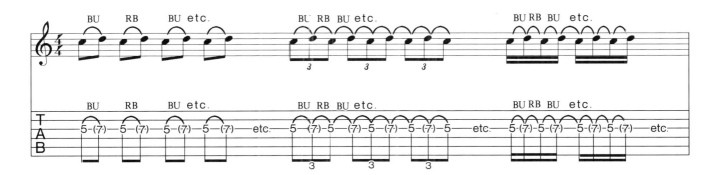

Project:

Listen to Jimi Hendrix, Stevie Ray Vaughan and B.B. King and try to imitate their vibrato.

If you want to pursue the techniques mentioned here further, I recommend my book "Rock Guitar Secrets" (AMA publishers).

Slide Guitar

Besides the already mentioned playing techniques there is another one that is pretty much inseparable from blues and has been there from the very beginnings: bottleneck or slide guitar playing.

Slide guitar was actually the first style of acoustic blues solo playing. Later, in the course of the development of rock and pop music, this style took it's place as well as an often used and much favored solo "coloration". Now before you go off smashing beer bottles to abuse your guitar with and getting frustrated by the sound that you get – and I speak here from personal experience – you should make a few preparations.

The right action.

To get the best results you should really adjust one guitar specially for slide. As this is generally an expensive way to go, the following "set up" suggestion is a good compromise. The most important thing with slide guitar playing is that the slide should not push the string all the way down to the fret, rather it should slide up and down the string unobstructed by the fret.

In a time at which most guitars are built to have as easy an action as possible, the normal factory "set up" just won't do the trick for slide. So, raise the action! The higher the action, the better for slide. As orientation point check out an acoustic guitar, as most of them have an action that can handle a bottle-neck. If you only have one guitar you'll have to find a compromise.

Beside this heavier strings (a .010 set or heavier) sound noticeably better. A possible compensation for the higher string tension would be tuning the guitar down a half step. Heavy strings and high action are usually a big change for many guitarists. Experiment around with different combinations and be careful not to stress out your left hand. And just as with "normal" guitar playing, there are no models of guitar that are particularily preferable for slide.

Different kinds of slides.

There are all sorts of different slides. They are made of either glass (hence the term "bottleneck") or metal and have many different sizes and weights. The two different materials have totally different sounds. Heavier metal slides sound somewhat better to me, but their weight, even for a "middling" string action and light strings are pretty difficult to manage for "slide" beginners. Lighter glass slides sound noticeably thinner in comparison and are easier to break. But even here, there are many different tastes and preferences. I, myself, often use a middle weight, blue lacquered metal slide. Here, too, you should try out a few different models til you find the one that suits your needs.

And now to the actual playing of slide guitar:

The left hand.

To get a more-or-less acceptable sound with the slide isn't as hard as one might think. The first question that comes to mind, of course, is which finger to put the slide on. But here as well, there is no absolutely clear answer. Although many guitarists wear the slide on their little finger in order to have the first three free for chording, many guitarists (e.g. Duane Allmann) put it on their ring finger. The important thing is that it doesn't get in the way of your playing.

The next and actually most important step is intonation. With a normally fretted note the tone is produced by having sufficient pressure on the string to press it down to the fret. Here it is pretty much the same if you press directly before the fret or maybe somewhere in the middle of the fret as long as there is enough pressure. But it's a different story with a slide! Here you'll have to position the slide exactly over the fret wire to get the right intonation for the note. As little as a millimeter too much in either direction can produce some pretty awful sounds. Here is an exercise for this:

This diagram illustrates an A blues scale as played exclusively on the g string. First fret every note with a free finger and then try to get it exactly with the slide. A lot will depend on using your ear, which is quicker than your eye in matters of intonation. Let your ear tell you when the tone is right.

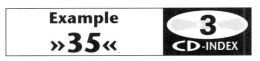

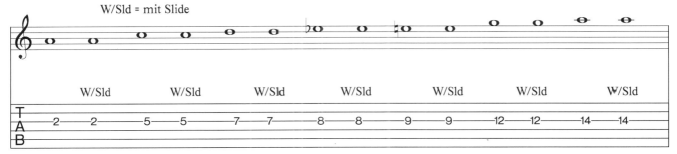

Project:

Try this on other strings.

With this simple technique you can already play "bluesy" licks. Do it!! You're probably getting a lot of extra string noise. In order to minimize this noise, simply take a left hand finger that's not being used and mute the strings behind the slide.

The Key to Success – Open Tunings

Although some guitarists such as Mike Bloomfield and the late Muddy Waters or Rick DeVito play slide guitar in standard tuning. It is usual to tune the guitar to a chord; this is referred to as an open tuning. Here are the two most often used open tunings: open G and open D.

Open G–Tuning

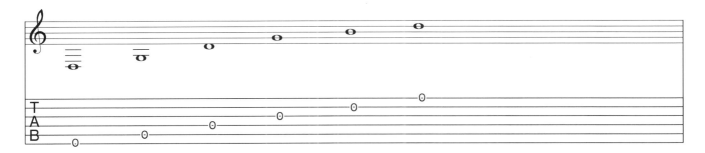

In order to get from standard tuning to open G follow these steps:

The low E is tuned down a whole step to D.
The A string is tuned down a whole step to G.
The D, G and B string remain the same.
The high E is tuned down a whole step to D.

Open D-Tuning

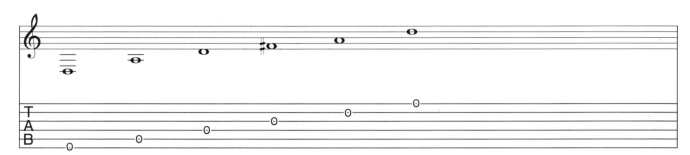

Here are the tuning steps that will take you to open D:

The E string is tuned a whole step down to D.
The A and D strings remain the same.
The G string is tuned a half step down to F#.
The B string is tuned a whole step down to A.
The high E string is tuned a whole step down to D.

With these open tunings, slide licks are definitely easier to play. You've already got a good sounding chord just by laying the slide over the strings like a bar, which helps quite a bit. You'll be able to see how this works "in action" in the up-coming solos in the style of Robert Johnson, Muddy Waters, Billy Gibbons and Duane Allman.

There are also variations on the above mentioned tunings: open A and open E. These vary from open G and open D only that they are a whole step higher each; they have the same relative configurations as, G and D. More information on this can be found in the book " Rock Guitar Harmonies" by Jürgen Kumlehn.

For jamming purposes, here is an A blues scale position in open G and one in open D.

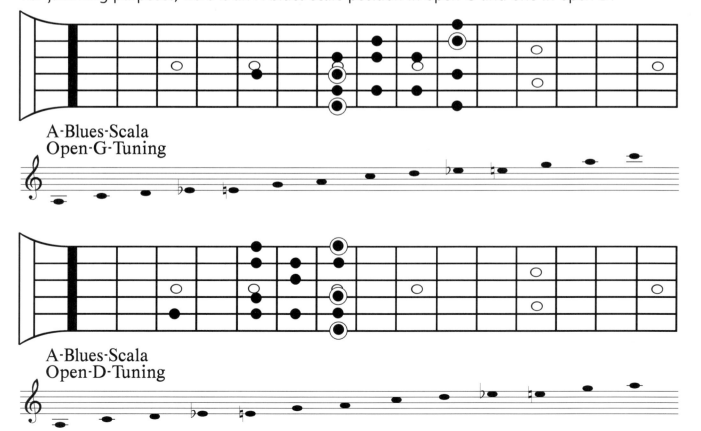

A-Blues-Scala
Open-G-Tuning

A-Blues-Scala
Open-D-Tuning

The right hand.

One possibility when playing slide is to play as usual with the pick, damping the unused strings with the ball of the hand. Many slide players, however, pick with their fingers. Besides being able to get a warmer sound, playing with your fingers offers the advantage of allowing you articulating better as well as enabling you to mute away the unwanted noises from the strings and slide. My hand position for this technique looks like this:

I use the ball of the hand to mute the lower strings using the thumb, index and middle finger to play or to mute the unplayed strings.

Phrasing

As long as you've gotten what I've shown you up til now half way under your belt the technical aspects of playing slide won't really be much of a problem for you. The point here is to play slide guitar in a way that sounds as un-technical as possible. The first step might be to add a bit of vibrato. As with "normal" playing, try experimenting here as well with different intensities. A further step might be trying to give your playing as much of a vocal quality as possible by singing out loud with your phrases. Try getting all the little details like lightly sliding into the notes, various bendings, rhythms etc.

Freddie King

The Note Material, Part 2

In order not to be limited to a single position of the minor pentatonic of blues scale you can also play these scales in other areas of the fingerboard. Here are five fingering patterns of the A–minor pentatonic blues scale which will enable you to jam all over the neck without playing a single wrong note. Start as you learn these patterns by keeping the pentatonic in mind and then, as a second step, add the ♭5 as a color note.

Pattern 1

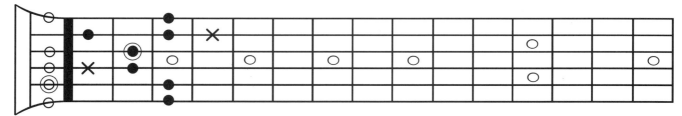

Pattern 2

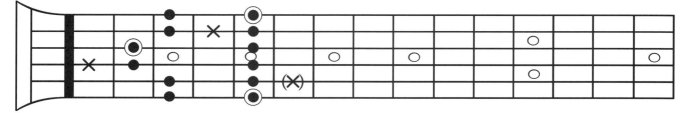

Pattern 3

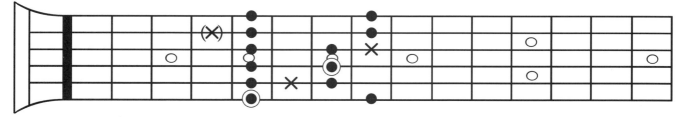

Pattern 4

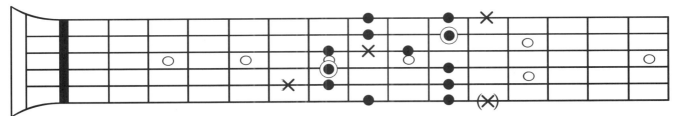

Pattern 5

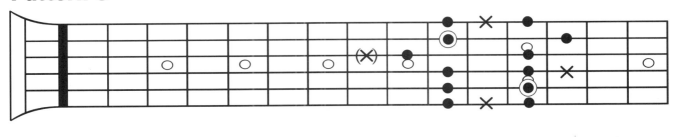

Project:

Record the blues form (dominant and minor) in A, E, G and B♭ and jam over it with the new scales.

Don't forget the quarter tone bends.

You can find blues licks on almost every rock, blues and pop LP as well as in my other books. Do it!

More scales for the dominant blues

The use of minor pentatonic gives more of a "true", primitive blues sound such as you might hear in the playing of Albert King, for example. Even though this scale, from a classical standpoint, could be seen as imperfect or even wrong I'd say that anything that sounds good can't really be wrong!

The minor pentatonic bluescale is not the only possibility for improvising over a dominant blues. A more B.B. King–like scale would be the major pentatonic. As with the minor pentatonic this scale is also without half tones.

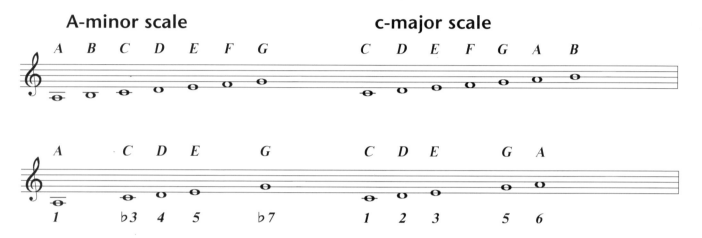

The A minor pentatonic contains exactly the same notes as the C major pentatonic, they simply begin on different notes. Getting from A minor to A major pentatonic is really quite simple: just transpose all A minor/C jamor scale patterns down a minor third and there you are in A major (or F♯ minor). In F♯ minor you can use the ♭5 as well of course.

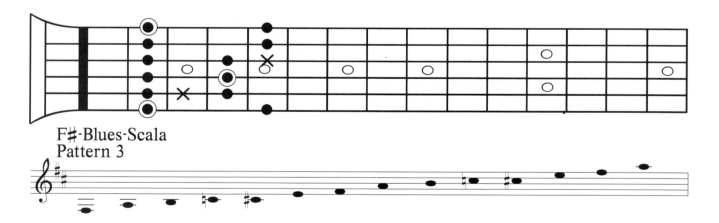

If you start on A instead of F♯, this scale offers you a minor third as well as a major third. If you now play this scale over an A⁷ chord, for example, you'll get a more cheerful, almost "country"-ish sound á la Albert Lee, Steve Morse or as we've already said, B.B. King.

After so much theory, it's time to get back to practice: which scale fits which chord?
This table can help you. It shows you which interval you get when you play both scales over the blues chords.

Minor pentatonic : A C D E G

over A^7 :	A = 1	C = $\sharp$9	D = 11	E = 5	G = $\flat$7
over D^7 :	A = 5	C = $\flat$7	D = 1	E = 9	G = 11
over E^7 :	A = 11	C = $\sharp$5	D = $\flat$7	E = 1	G = $\sharp$9

Major pentatonic : A B C# E F#

over A^7 :	A = 1	B = 9	C$\sharp$ = 3	E = 5	F$\sharp$ = 13
over D^7 :	A = 5	B = 13	C$\sharp$ = 7	E = 9	F$\sharp$ = 3
over E^7 :	A = 11	B = 5	C$\sharp$ = 13	E = 1	F$\sharp$ = 9

Looking at this table you can see what effect the two scales have when played over the three chords.

The most "round" sounding combinations are those with as few alterations as possible ($\flat$5, $\sharp$5, $\flat$9, $\sharp$9). Alterations are chromatically changed chordal extension notes (options), "tension" notes that for the inexperienced ear can sound a bit strange. The fewer alterations, the smoother the sound. You can also see that the A major pentatonic produces a major 7th over the D^7. The "sourest and wrongest" notes that you can play over this chord.
Remember that you can also add the blue note to these scales.

Good scale choices for the dominant blues might be:

for the primitive blues sound á la Albert King:
          A minor pentatonic / blues scale over all chords:

For the more melodic, rounder blues sound á la B.B. King:
          A major pentatonic (plus $\flat$3) over A^7 and E^7,
          A minor pentatonic over D^7.

Project:

Play major pentatonics (D and E) over the D^7 and E^7. How does that sound?

How does the D blues scale over D^7 and E blues scale over E^7 sound?

One question that of course comes to mind is what does one play on a minor blues? For the minor blues try these scale combinations: over all three chords (Am, Dm, Em or E^7) play the A blues scale.

Play the blues scale of each one of the chords (i.e. A blues over Am, D blues over Dm, E blues over Em or E^7).

Play the E minor pentatonic over the Am.

So how does it all sound?

Remember: the choice is determined by your taste.

The Blues Feeling

Now that you have all of these basic and important elements at your command there is one left that we haven't discussed: the so-called blues feeling.

In blues and all blues-related music styles (rock, metal etc.) it is of greatest importance to play with the right attitude or feeling; this separates it markedly from the more stiff, disciplined European classical music.

Here there is less emphasis on technically perfect execution of a piece of music, and more on the expression of feelings through the instrument. With blues this mostly means pain, worry and sadness.

There is an expression that comes from (classical) music theory: dirty intonation. Blues is not cleanly intonated. It is played definitely and intentionally dirty in order to "blow away the pain". In terms of technique, all the devices that one can use to achieve this (quarter tone bends, slides etc.) are those which "serious" music tends to disapprove of.

They can all be learned. Transforming your feelings into music is something that cannot. We are fortunately all different.

So that we don't get too abstract with all these ideas, here is a worked-over version of the solo that we started with:

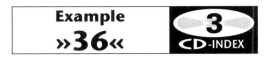

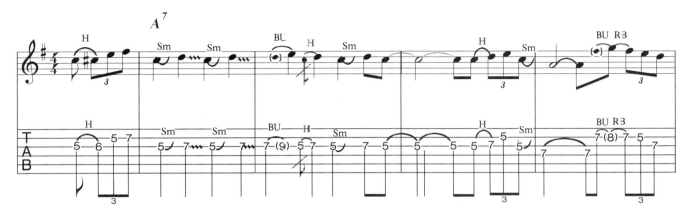

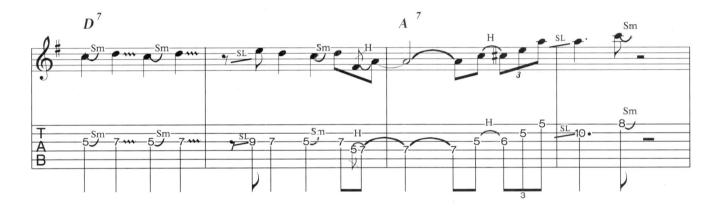

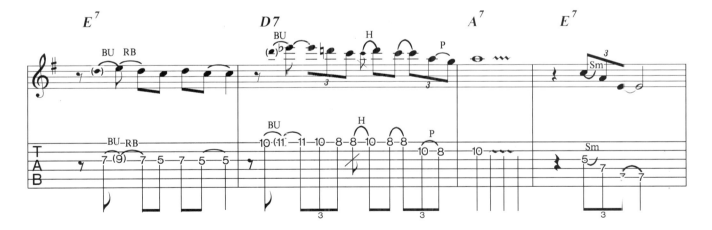

Whats different now?

In general I've played the solo with more feeling and drive. In addition I've added small phrasing details like small bends, hammer-ons and slides to most of the notes. Whereas in the first version there were numerous empty spaces, I've now added small fills. An interesting effect is the octave transposition of the phrase in measure 10.

Chapter 5
Easy and Early Blues Styles – Country and Chicago Blues

After so much theoretical information about blues, its about time we get down to the nitty–gritty: simple solos in the style of the old blues masters. As in my opinion the construction and overall contour of the solo is a matter of greatest importance I've built most of the licks and riffs in this book into complete solos. Besides many of the licks of the "old masters" are so unspectacular that they are only effective in context. This does not mean, of course, that you should only play the solo as it is. On the contrary, you should mix phrases, lines or measures of different solos all over the place. This will give you solos that have some of your own personality in them. Besides, a single solo obviously cannot completely define a musician's style. All the solos presented in this book are intended to give you a good look at the style of the particular guitarist. On the other hand, through comparison and a comprehensive look at the different styles and blues interpretations, they will enable you to see the many possibilities offered by the blues. The different solos should give you a chance to sample the many different ways of serving the blues. As we said at the beginning, in feeling oriented music such as blues, your ear and a lot of getting into the music will help you most of all in becoming a good blues guitarist. It also is important while you learn these solos is not just to have your eyes glued to the written music but also to make use of the CD. But now lets get on to the music.

Robert Johnson
Style Solo

King of the Delta Blues

The mythical Robert Johnson (1911 – 1938) appears as the first guitarist in this style unit. Influenced by country-bluesers like Charlie Patton, Son House and Willie Brown, he was actually the first blues "star" in music history. Decades after his mysterious death he still influenced generations of blues guitarists, from Muddy Waters to Eric Clapton. To this day his most famous songs, such as "Crossroads Blues", "Ramblin on my Mind"and"Terraplane Blues", belong to the great blues classics.

About the solo

For the country blues of Robert Johnson, a few things are quite important:

1)   Playing with the fingers or with a thumb pick .

2)   A pretty hard attack; high action and heavy strings were the norm in those days

3)   An alternation of slide parts and parts fretted with the fingers

4)   A pretty free interpretation of 4/4 time and 12 bar form. Johnson would often steal a quarter beat here or add an extra there, changing the form to fit his mood.

Robert Johnson's guitar was probably tuned to open G tuning (D–G–D–G–B–D); most of his licks and fills are built on chord forms associated with this tuning. In order to fit each song to his voice, he often used a capo. The intonation in the slide parts is made somewhat easier by using lots of vibrato.

To get the sound of Robert Johnson more important than the guitar (any acoustic guitar with steel strings will do) is the way of playing. In the slide passages, strike the strings downwards with the thumb or pluck every string with the fingers.

In the rhythm parts, hit all the open strings downwards with the fore and middlefingers, all unaccented beats with an upward motion with the back of the thumbnail (back thumbing).

In this solo, slide inserts are alternated with rhythm parts. Right in keeping with Robert Johnson's style, I've added a quarter note in measure 6. Also interesting is that in measures 9 and 10, two measures of D^7 appear where usually a D^7–C^7 progression is found.

Example »37«

4 CD-INDEX

⚠ **in Open G-Tuning** (see page 49)

Discography: Fortunately the complete works of Robert Johnson can be found on one double LP or CD from Columbia Records.

Muddy Waters
Style Solo

The father of the electric blues

Whereas the delta blues of Robert Johnson and his contemporaries was played exclusively with acoustic guitars, Muddy Waters (1945 – 1983) is largely responsible for the electrification of the blues guitar. Strongly influenced by Son House he gave blues a new dimension and established the sound of Chicago blues with cutting slide played on his telecaster and his blues big band sound with piano, harmonica, bass, drums and rhythm guitar as well as lyrics full of sex, superstition and voodoo. As the first black blues guitarist ever to tour in Europe he had a strong influence on british guitarists in the 60's such as Clapton, Alexis Korner or the Rolling Stones, who even got their name from one of his songs. Other Muddy Waters classics are: "Rollin' and Tumblin'", "I'm your Hoochie Coochie Man" and "Baby please don't go"

About the solo

To get this sound, a telecaster style instrument sounds best, as this was the model that Waters mostly played. Besides this it's important to know that he played with a thumb pick. This solo, is also in open G tuning although Muddy Waters in his later years mostly played in standard tuning. In this solo one can again see how simple a good blues solo can be. In blues, less is usually more.

Example »38«  **in Open G-Tuning** (see page 49)

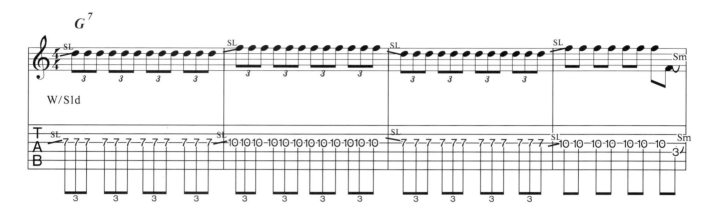

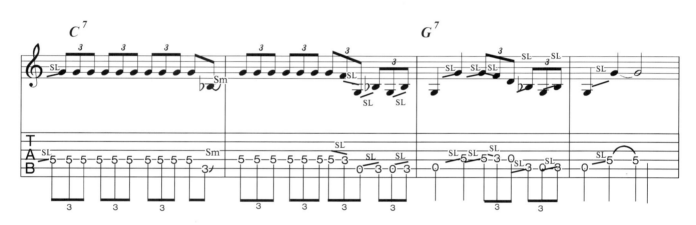

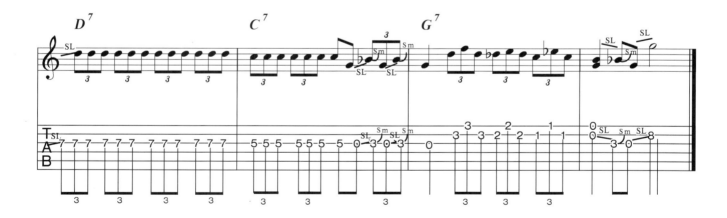

Discography: There are a number of "greatest hits" albums. They've almost all got the same tunes on them, so it doesn't really matter which one you choose.

John Lee Hooker
Style Solo

Born to Boogie

Everybody knows him, the old bluesman in the cult film "The Blues Brothers" playing his "how-how-how" poker-facedly into the camera.

He's John Lee Hooker, the master of the boogie. In contrast to the old blues masters that we've looked at up till now, Hooker began his involvement with music at the end of the 30's with gospel songs. To avoid problems he released over 70 singles under a dozen pseudonyms between 1949 and 1953 after his first hit "Crawling Kingsnake". His 1962 hit, "Boom, Boom" is today still a popular cover tune. After a number of years' abstinence from public perfomance he made an enormous comeback in the early 90's with two brilliant albums, "The Healer" and "Mr. Lucky" the success of which cannot be credited only to the incredible line-up of guest super-stars.

About the solo

What's special about John Lee Hooker's style is his simplicity and his boogie rhythm that one finds in many of his songs. As he often plays tunes in which there are relatively few chord changes this puts an extra emphasis on their rhythmic components. The form is also pretty unusual: a 16 bar form with a four bar intro.

Like many other guitarists form the first generation of blues guitarists, Hooker uses open G or open A tuning.

In the following solo you can find numerous characteristics of John Lee's style. Besides the typical quarter note triplet breaks such as those in measures 9/10 and 15/16 the off-beat accented rhythm makes this chorus "happen". Here I've wrapped up a few different variations on this theme into a single groove.

To get the sound as close as possible, play all single notes as well as the breaks with a downstroke of the thumb and everything else with upstrokes of the index finger. But be careful: as this also sounds better when you play with a hard attack, you can develop blisters pretty quickly.

Example »39« CD-INDEX 4 ⚠ in Open G-Tuning (see page 49)

Discography: From John Lee Hooker there is also a very good compilation LP: The Ultimate Collection 1948– 1990.

B.B. King
Style Solo

The King of the blues

He is called the "king of the blues" and for good reason ... his influence on the guitarists of the post war generations is undeniable. Few artists in this genre have been honored (among other credits: an honorary doctoral degree and a Grammy for "The Thrill is gone") and received such glowing critical acclaim as has B.B. King. His playing and singing style has, in fact, influenced almost anyone today directly or indirectly who has anything to do with the blues. In the course of his long career, B.B. has not only played pure blues but has also been active and influential in pop music with his own unmistakeable style.

About the solo:

B.B. King is known for his somewhat more cheerful presentation of the blues in which he often uses the major pentatonic for his solos. You can find three example solos in my book "Masters of Rock Guitar". For this reason I'm offering an example in minor here, in which you can see the call and response style quite clearly.

Notice how much space is left between the phrases.

Example »40« **4 CD-INDEX**

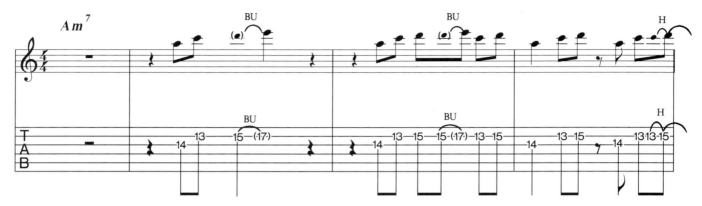

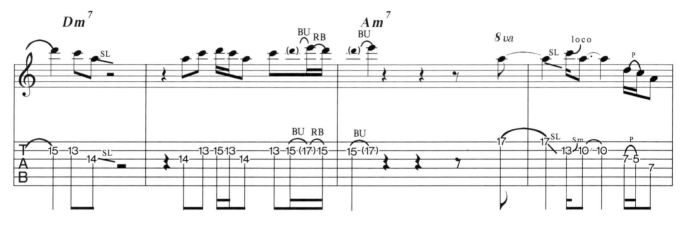

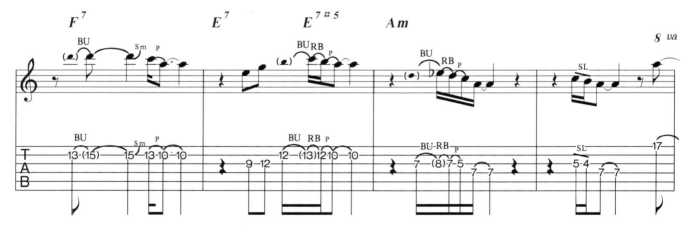

Discography: B.B. Kings concerts always have a particularly "up" vibe to them, for which reason I highly recommend live recordings like "Live at San Quentin" or "Live at the Apollo".

Project:

I've consciously played all the solos on the CD until now in the styles and with the sounds of the old masters. The solos sound good as well, however, if you play them with more modern sounds and more "attitude".

Albert King
Style Solo

Born under a bad sign

"Born under a bad sign"... thats the name of one of Albert Kings (1924 – 1992) biggest hits. Covered by people like Robben Ford and Pat Travers it has become one of the greatest blues classics. "Born Under a Bad Sign" could also have been the subtitle for the life of this lumbering old blues master. In contrast to the other "king" of the blues, B.B., he never managed to have much commercial success. After many years without a record contract he returned to the limelight through his guest appearance on Gary Moore's

LP "Still Got the Blues". Despite his commercial misfortunes his guitar style can be heard almost everywhere. His influence can be easily recognized in the playing of Stevie Ray Vaughan who, aside from being influenced by Jimi Hendrix, leans heavily on Albert King's raw, direct blues playing.

About the solo:
To be honest, there is not an unlimited quantity of Albert King licks. He managed, however, with his unbelievable phrasing, to make his limited vocabulary of licks always sound fresh and interesting. As he picked using the flesh of his thumb only, hitting the strings pretty roughly, every note sounds different (as in the playing of Jeff Beck who also plays with only his fingers). Beside this, Albert King's sound is defined by his nuance- filled bends that range from quarter to two-and-a-half tones in size. An additional factor is that he was a left-hander who played a normal guitar upside-down.

In the following solo I've joined numerous short fragments together into a complete solo. Although this solo has a similar construction to the B.B. King solo it sounds totally different owing to the completely different techniques of the two guitarists.

Example »41«

Discography: Here are a few good tips:

Albert King – Travelling to California
– The lost Sessions
– Red House

Stage 2

Blues Rock Styles

Chapter 6
The basis of the blues, part 2

Now that we've spent the first five chapters looking at early blues and the fundamental components of the blues, we are now going to go on to refine some of the rhythmic and harmonic aspects of the music.

Blues harmony, part 2
or the modes and the blues

In order to extend the repertoire of "note material" that we've developed for jamming over the blues we can turn to the old so-called modes.

As I've already described the applications of modal theory in my book "Rock Guitar Secrets" in detail I'm going to make my presentation of this material here a bit shorter.

Scales can be described by their intervallic construction or the distribution of half and whole steps, i.e. their positions within the scale.

This is a major scale (or the ionian mode) in c:

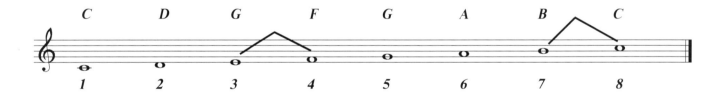

As you can see, the half steps lie between steps 3/4 and 7/8. This happens in all major scale regardless of which note they start on. Now if one begins the scale on a different note, the positions of the half and whole steps change.

If one starts on each one of the other notes, the result is six new scales: the remaining modes of C major.

The ionian system.

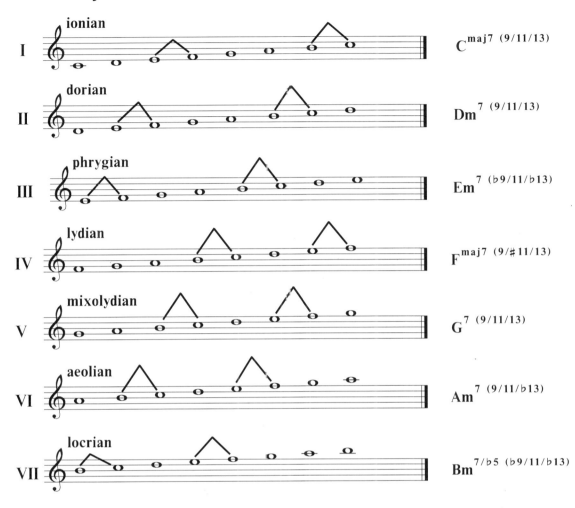

Each mode is associated with one of the diatonic chords, for which the mode is the correct scale choice for improvising over that chord.

Modes in the dominant blues.

As you can see in the diagram above the diatonic chord built on the fifth step of the C major scale is the G^7 chord, accompanied by its scale the G mixolydian. As all examples in this book until now have been in A, lets transpose everything over to A:

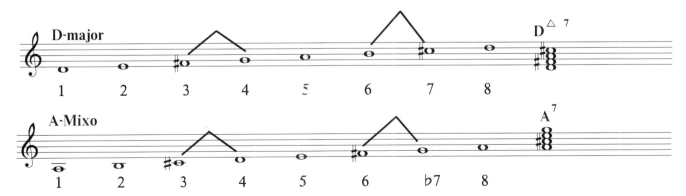

The chord A^7 and the A mixolydian scale are now the diatonic chord and scale built on the fifth step. Beside the major and minor pentatonic in A this scale now becomes the third possible choice for a scale to play over the A^7 chord.

Here are the five fingering positions for the A–mixolydian (=D major). When you learning these new fingerings try to use the notes of the A major pentatonic as a basis, thinking the g and d as added notes.

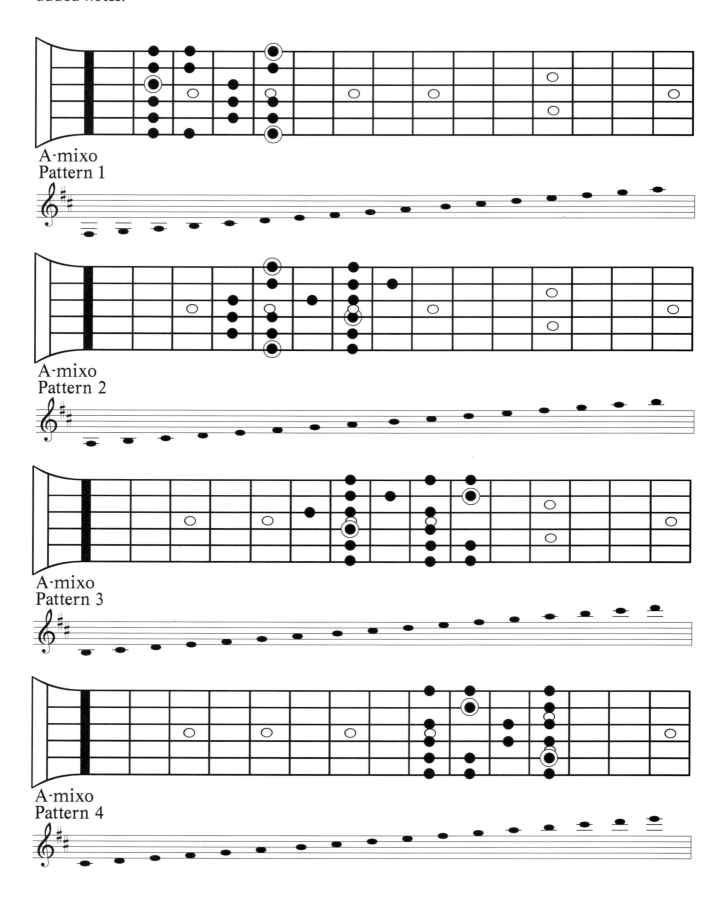

A-mixo
Pattern 1

A-mixo
Pattern 2

A-mixo
Pattern 3

A-mixo
Pattern 4

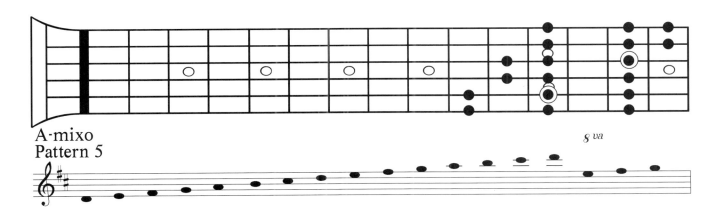

A-mixo
Pattern 5

Of course, in a blues you'll not only encounter A^7 but D^7 and E^7 as well. This is how we get the mixolydian scales for these chords.

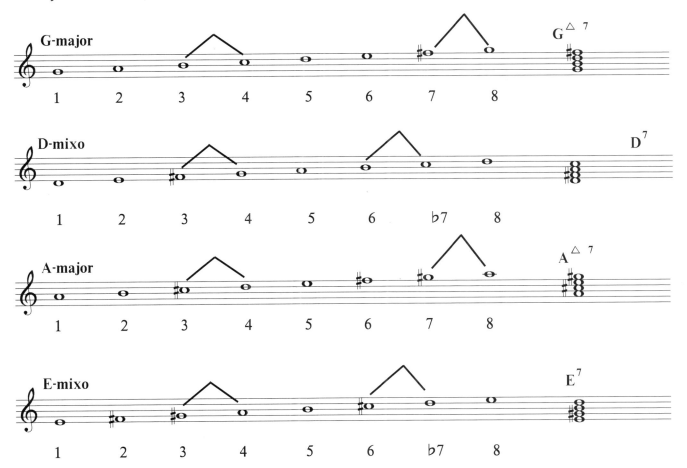

You can probably guess what's coming next: slide the positions in the scale diagram above over to D and E mixo.

Project:

It's jammin' time again!

Play a blues in A and improvise over every chord with its mixolydian scale.

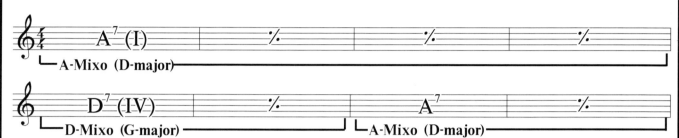

How about trying this out with a different blues form or another key?

For modal freaks: You can also look at this scale scheme from the standpoint of the pitch axis system:

A^7 : A-mixo   (= D-major)
D^7 : A-dorian   (= G-major = D-mixo)
E^7 : A-ionian   (=A-major   = E-mixo)

(see Rock Guitar Secrets).

So, how does that sound? A bit too slick, huh?

The reason for this is that in the mixolydian scale neither the ♭5 or the minor third (with the potential to bend to the blues third) are present. Besides which, you might also be playing a bit too "scale oriented", something which happens easily with this kind of scale.

In short: the real, pentatonic blues sound is missing. What now?

If we wanted to add the missing notes to the fingering positions that we've already got, that would get complicated and hard to get under control. The real solution to this problem is much simpler – Here are the A pentatonic and the A blues scale.

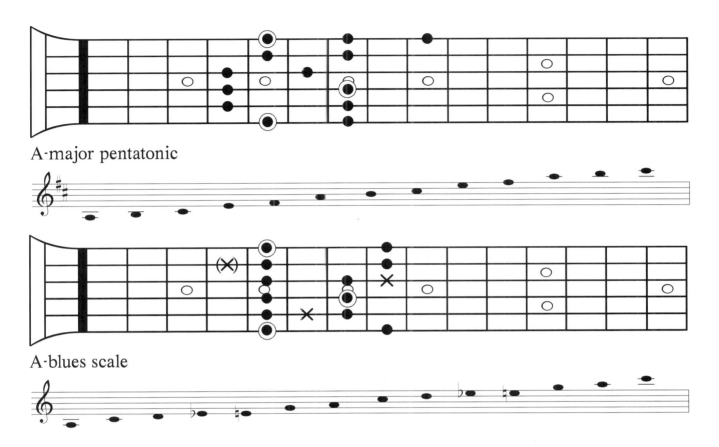

A-major pentatonic

A-blues scale

These are the notes that can be played over A⁷.
If you now mix both scales together you come up with the following scale, named the "hip scale" by Paul Gilbert.

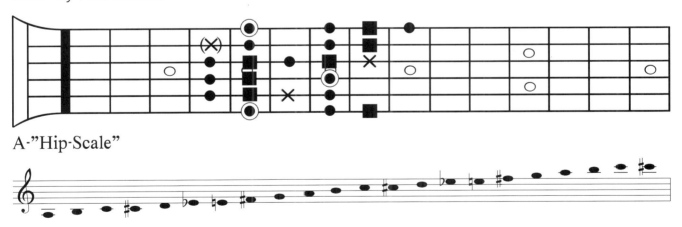

A-"Hip-Scale"

Here it's important to see this series of notes not as a new scale but as the sum of two scales in one position.

This works as well, of course in D and E.

Here is the hip scale in D and E in the 5th position.

Here too, try not to see this fingering position as a new scale but more as a combination of two familiar positions (major pentatonic and blues scale) rolled up into one.

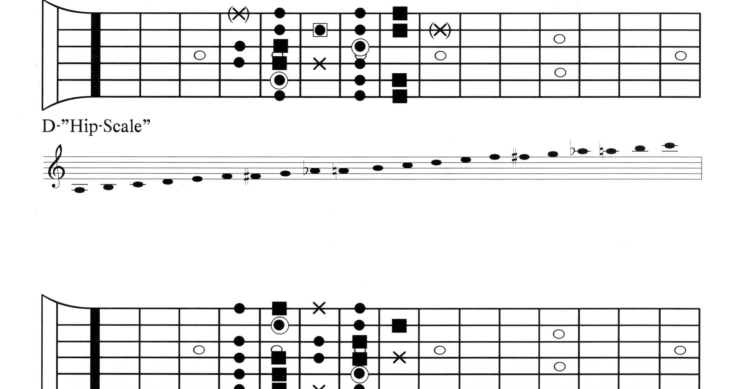

D-"Hip-Scale"

E-"Hip-Scale"

As you can see, with the help of this concept you can use up to 9 of the 12 possible notes over every chord when jamming. In order not to get lost, always resolve to a chord tone (1–3–5–7). They should be the central, "home bases" for your improvisation where you can relax, while the other notes serve as connections and color-notes.

Here are the A^7, D^7 and E^7 arpeggios in the 5th position.

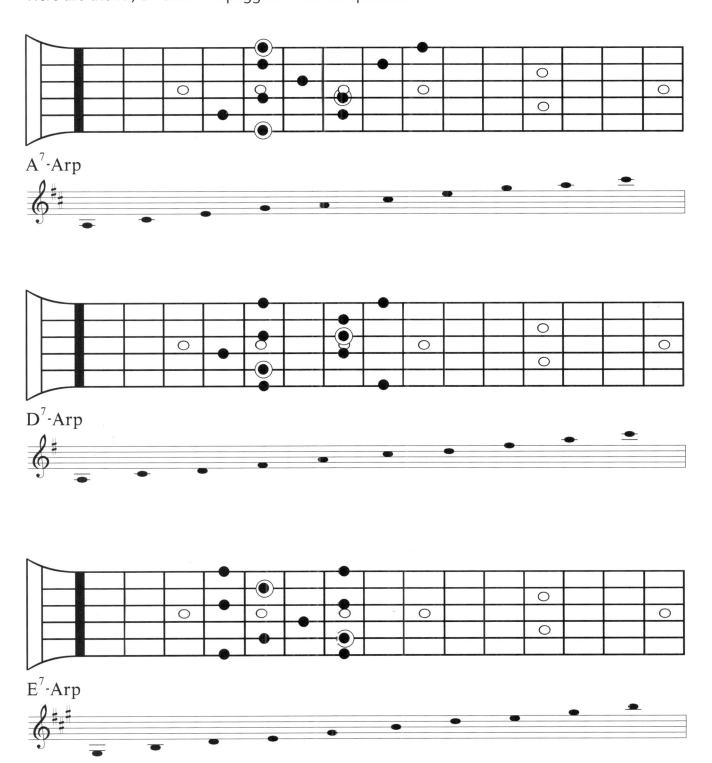

A^7-Arp

D^7-Arp

E^7-Arp

All you have to do in order to have the mixolydian scale and the two typical tension notes ($\flat$5 and blues third) at your fingertips is to combine the major pentatonic and the blues scale in the same position on the fingerboard. When jamming, alternate between the two in the same part of the neck, always resolving to the chord tones of what ever chord you're playing over. This way, you can further use your pentatonic licks and phrasing but also have many more notes available.

Example
»42«

Project:

Combine the D major pentatonic and the blues scale in other positions on the fingerboard.

Don't forget the chord tones!

Don't forget the blues third!

Modes in minor blues.

With minor blues the problems are not as easy to solve as with the minor or minor 7th chord you have a choice of three different available scales: dorian, phrygian and aeolian (see diagram p. 71).

Curiously, however, the chords from the diagram that go with these scales are exactly the chords that are found in the "original" form of the minor blues: Am^7 (I), Dm^7 (IV) and Em^7 (V).

Another possible way of getting more notes that could be used would simply be to play a C major scale over all three chords. From a modal standpoint, you would be playing the aeolian over Am^7, the dorian over Dm^7 and the phrygian over the Em^7.

DO IT!!

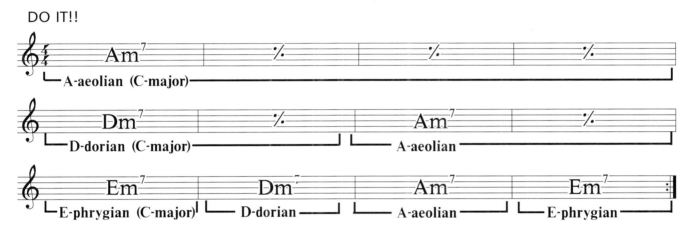

Should you find this sounds boring: things will get a bit more interesting if you start trying out other scale possibilities over each chord. I myself find the phrygian mode particularly "un-bluesy" and I suggest not to use it. The dorian played over every chord sounds a little more angular to me and for this reason more interesting.

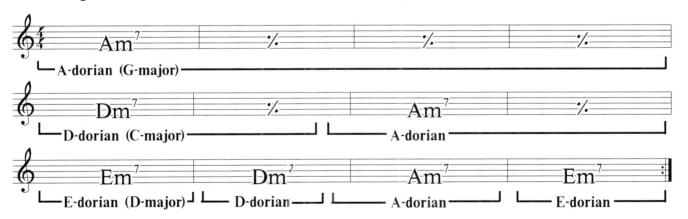

But what happens when the V chord is a dominant 7th (E^7)? The first thought that comes to mind might be to use the mixolydian scale. In my opinion the difference between the sound of E mixo and the minor scales is so extreme that this choice should be ruled out. To get a unified sound we'll have to find a scale that

> a) has E^7 as a diatonic chord and
> b) is not too different note-wise from A dorian or A aeolian.

This scale is A harmonic minor.

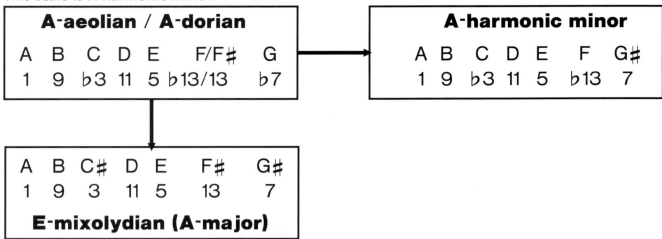

For more information on the A harmonic minor scale, I recommend, once again, my book "Rock Guitar Secrets".

Here is a simple solo using the above mentioned scales.

Example »43«   5 CD-INDEX

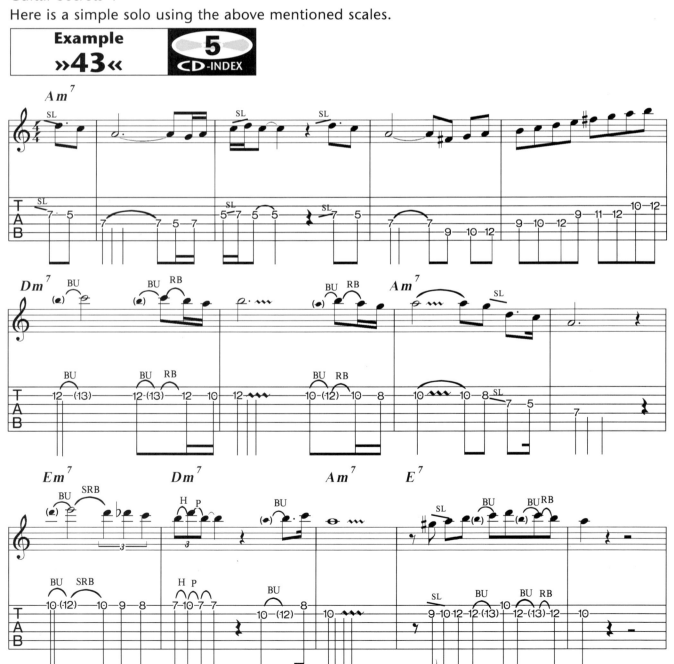

To wrap things up here is a small table showing all the chord scale combinations we have encoutered until now.

Dominant-Blues

A^7	D^7	E^7
A-minor pentatonic	A-minor pentatonic	A-minor pentatonic
A blues scale	A blues scale	A blues scale
A-major pentatonic	D-major pentatonic	E-major pentatonic
F# blues scale	D-minor pentatonic	E-minor pentatonic
A-mixolydian	D-mixolydian	E-mixolydian
A-"hip scale"	D-"hip scale"	E-"hip scale"

Minor-Blues

$Am^{(7)}$	$Dm^{(7)}$	$Em^{(7)}$
A-minor pentatonic	A-minor pentatonic	A-minor pentatonic
A blues scale	A blues scale	A blues scale
E-minor pentatonic	D-minor pentatonic	E-minor pentatonic
A-aeolian	D-dorian	E-phrygian
A-dorian		E-dorian

E^7: E-phrygian dominant (A-harmonic minor)

Project:

Don't panic!

So ... you've heard of arpeggios before, haven't you?

You can of course use the arps of the various modes over the chords. Do it!

The rhythm of blues, part 2
or – groove or die!

Although you can cover almost every area in traditional blues with the basic rhythmic ideas described in chapter I.(p.17/18), in order to be able to analyse the various blues rock styles in the coming chapter, we'll have to learn one more important term: the double-time shuffle, commonly refered to as "the boogie".

In a normal shuffle, two eighth notes are swung in a "triplet"-ish way so that instead of a stiff eighth note rhythm a grooving shuffle is produced.

With a boogie rhythm the same thing happens, but this time twice as fast (double time). Instead of eighth notes, the sixteenth notes are "shuffled".

If you now play the 2nd and 4th note of each group almost inaudibly, the effect will be that of very strongly grooving straight eighth notes which are particularly hard to play at slow tempos. In this manner, slower straight binary rhythms are supplied with a double time foundation in order to get them really rolling. By the way, this is a trick that Glenn Miller and other swing masters of the 40's and 50's knew and that almost all rap and hip-hop acts use and that is indispensable to various other musical styles for getting that certain "swing".

The same thing works with a normal shuffle by the way, even for very slow quarter notes. This rhythm is often used by many R + B influenced bands like ZZ Top and Aerosmith. To understand this new rhythm better I'd recommend listening to the following songs:

Aerosmith : "Rag Doll" (Permanent Vacation)
"Love in an elevator" (Pump)
"Walk This way"

Joe Satriani : "Satch boogie" - Intro (Surfing with the alien)

Glenn Miller : "Chattanoga choo choo"

Chapter 7
Bluesrock of the 60's and 70's

As we've seen in chapter V the blues began pretty simple, although you've certainly noticed that it is not easy to sound like one of the old blues masters or to reproduce their groove and tone. These aspects of blues guitar are certainly the most difficult and as I've often said, using your ears and playing a lot of blues are really the best learning methods available.

The following chapter is another unit on blues styles; this time, however, we will be concentrating on a number of the more modern guitar hot-shots.

We'll begin with the guitarists of the 60's and 70's all of who, in their youth, were influenced by the musicians that we encoutered in Chapter V.

The basic difference between these guitarists and their idols was that they were often white and developed blues in more of a rock direction; they experienced blues as an extremely important source but were influenced by many other styles as well.

This second generation of strongly blues influenced guitarists, are players like Jeff Beck, Michael Bloomfield, Peter Green, Jimi Hendrix, Jimmy Page, Duane Allman, Richie Blackmore, The Rolling Stones, Carlos Santana and many others offer a musical experience that's well worth a listen.

As representatives of this era I've chosen three guitarists with quite different styles: Jimi Hendrix, Eric Clapton and Duane Allmann.

Besides the licks that appear in this book another important element in this style was the use of repeating patterns, a number of which can be found in my first book "Masters of Rock Guitar".

Jimi Hendrix
Style Solo

Playing the Red House Blues

Jimi Hendrix can certainly be considered to be the inventor of modern rock guitar. His playing, his relatively short but meteoric career as well as his effect on his audience and the following generation of guitarists have never been equalled, with the possible exception of Eddie van Halen.

After three hit albums that were, by the standards of the times and today's as well, guitaristic milestones and a number of historical concert appearances (for example Woodstock) he fell into a musical and personal vacuum. On the 18th of September, 1970, Hendrix died in Kensington, England; the causes of his death are still unclear.

About the solo

Aside from the many hits from his LPs, Hendrix played a very personal blues, which kept taking on new aspects during the course of his career: the "Red House Blues". This song was with him during the entire time in which he was active as a performer. It is the Hendrix blues. On the occasion of the 20th anniversary of his death, a CD was released with 6 different versions of this song. This CD is, in my opinion, the best recording of Hendrix that one can hear.

The following solo is in the "Red House" style. It contains some of his most typical blues licks. You should give yourself some time to study this solo .. it is pretty difficult. I've also tried on the CD to play around with the beat like Jimi did. You should use the written music as an orientation point and then try to get the phrasing from the CD. Pay special attention to dynamics, they're very important. When playing the loud and fast passages, you should use a pretty hard attack.

From a harmonic standpoint nothing unusual happens here. Occasionally a 9th or 6th is added to the normal blues scale. This solo gets its life from the phrasing.

Example »44«

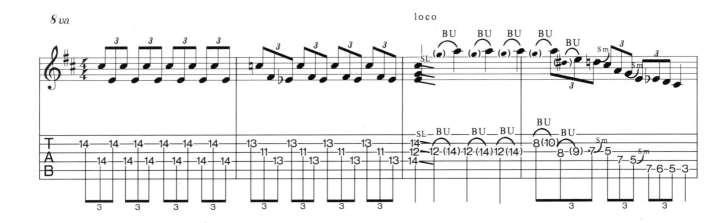

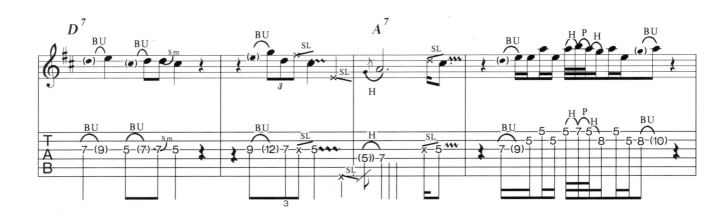

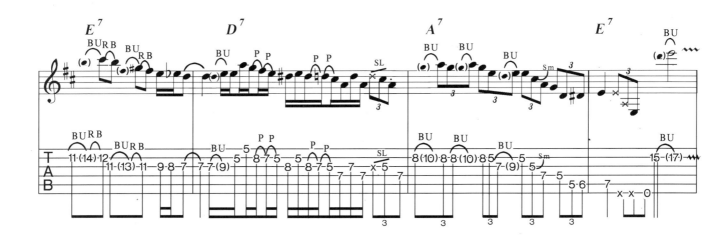

Discography: Besides the bestsellers: "Are you exeperienced?", "axis:Bold as love" and "electric Ladyland", you should definitely have this record: **Jimi Hendrix** Reference Library - Variations of a theme: Red House.

Eric Clapton
Style Solo

Standing at the Crossroads

"Eric Clapton is God" – this message could be read on the T-shirts of many Eric Clapton fans in the mid 60's. Although one could argue this assertion Clapton has undeniably played a leading role in the development of rock guitar. He was a figurehead of the "British invasion", the wave of strongly blues-influenced English bands that came out of the 60's. After his rise to fame and almost legendary status through his work with bands like John Mayall's Bluesbreakers, Cream and Derek and the Dominoes which he influenced greatly with his virtuoso blues rock playing he lapsed into a period of drug problems starting in the early 70's during which he almost didn't play. This phase lasted into the mid 80's. Although during this period the guitar played an unimportant role for him his fortunes have improved since then and "Slow Hand" has begun to play more and better than ever.

About the solo

There is also a very famous blues from Clapton: the Cream version of the old Robert Johnson song "Crossroads", markedly different from the original. In contrast to most other blues "hits" this tune is a relatively fast, straight ahead rock number containing some really hot Clapton guitar soloing. These solos are much more fluid and more oriented towards long melodic ideas than those of his contemporaries. His technique, rhythm and vibrato were also more sophisticated, controlled and ornate than those of the other guitarists.

His choice of notes and how he applied them were also very much his own. Clapton often played the mix of major and minor pentatonic, mentioned in chapter VI, which gives his playing a great deal of drama and color. While playing the solo pay special attention to which chord tones Clapton resolves to.

The following are two choruses in "Crossroads style" The first is more rhythm guitar oriented where as the second contains a couple of cool Clapton blues licks.

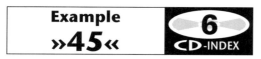

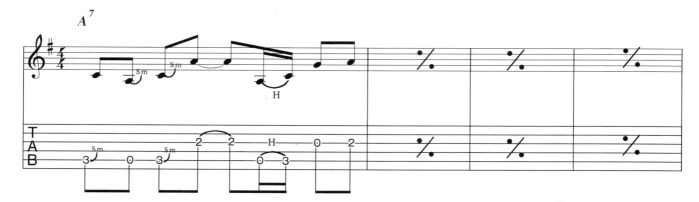

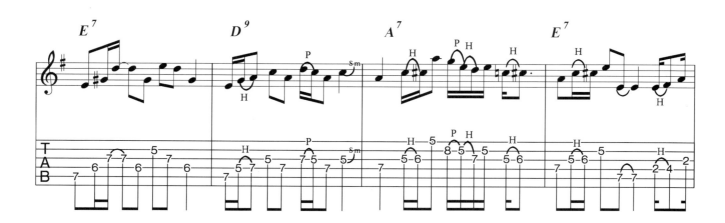

Discography: Originally on Cream's "Wheels of Fire", "Crossroads" can be found on almost all
Clapton samplers.

Duane Allman
Style Solo

Statesboro Blues

When Duane Allman died on 10/29/71 at the age of 24 the world of guitar lost one of its greatest talents. As with so many, Jimi Hendrix, Randy Rhoads or later on Stevie Ray Vaughan, he left behind only a handful of recordings from which it was clear what a tremendous creative potential he'd had. Duane Allman, together with his brother Gregg, were the musical head of the Allman Brothers, a band which since its foundation in 1964 stood as the epitome of southern rock. They had a mega–hit with the instrumental "Jessica" some time after Duane's death. Their album "Live at the Fillmore East" is regarded today as a rock classic. On this record Duane Allman's slide guitar broke into a new era for this style of playing. Allman also managed to write guitar history as a side man. Besides numerous other jobs he played as a guest artist with Eric Clapton's band at the time "Derek and the Dominoes" on whose album "Layla and other assorted love songs" he played slide parts unequalled to this day.

About the solo

The following solo is in the key of D and is in the style of "Statesboro Blues". You might recognize the beginning riff from Gary Moore's playing. It shows how a classic riff that was already played in the 30's can be interpreted in a new way. The solo is a slide solo in open E tuning (see p. 49). In my opinion, this tuning isn't quite so "bluesy" as open G, but sounds more cheerful and melodic. The licks are oriented, as is so often the case in slide playing, towards bar–like chord positions. Particularly interesting is the lick in the 9th measure. Here you should pay more attention to the phrasing and the attitude than if every note is perfectly intonated.

In order to articulate as well as possible I'd recommend that you set the pick aside and play with your fingers, as Duane did.

Example
»46«

 in Open E-Tuning

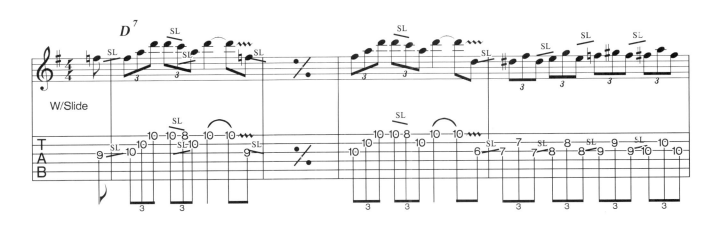

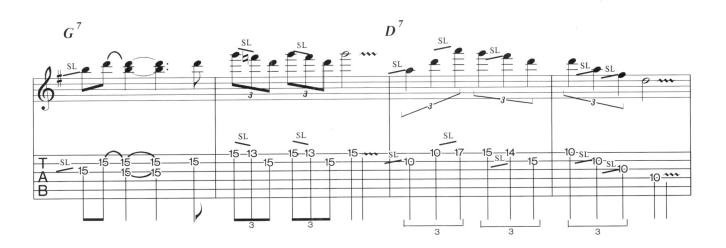

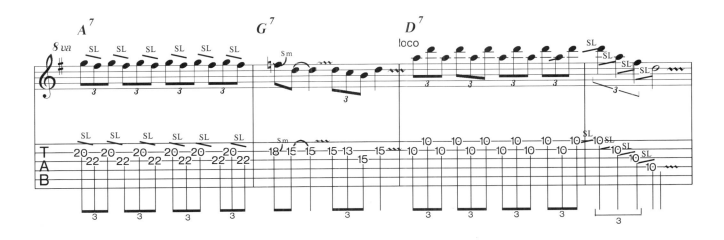

Discography: to get a comprehensive view of Duane Allman's work, I recommend the following sampler: The **Allmann Brothers** – The road goes forever

Chapter 8

Texas Blues

In contrast to the cooler, more solid, traditional Chicago blues the Texas blues is characterized by its temperament. The first important representative of this style was T–Bone Walker who early in his career made clear the main difference between the two blues scenes. He combined expressive, high energy blues guitar playing with a spectacular stage act in which he would, for example, play with the guitar behind his head or between his legs. With this show he set milestones in stage performance that influenced other Texas blues guitarists like Buddy Guy, Stevie Ry Vaughan or rock legend Jimi Hendrix. So, in addition to the fact that Texas blues is a bit more raw and arggessive in sound than Chicago blues, the main difference is the preference for flipped–out costumes and wild showmanship on stage.

For this style, I've chosen two guitar "greats": Stevie Ray Vaughan and Billy Gibbons.

Stevie Ray Vaughan
Style Solo

The Sky is crying

A cry of sadness was heard through the guitar world as, on the morning of August 21, 1990, it was reported that in the previous night the greatest white blues guitarist of all time had died in a helicopter crash.

Stevie Ray Vaughan had managed to combine the influences of Albert King, Jimi Hendrix and the long tradition of Texas blues and earned himself a place in the line-up of the most important blues guitarists of the century.

His big break-through came in 1983 as sideman on David Bowie's "Let's Dance" album. This record and his fantastic first solo LP, "Texas Flood", which came out in the same year, made him the talk of the guitar world. Almost overnight the local Texas git-picker became a super star, a living guitar legend ... a reputation that he justified with each new LP.

Only his friends saw the dark side: under permanent pressure with recordings and tours, he became heavily dependent on alcohol and other drugs for a few years. In 1989, shortly before recording his "In Step" album, considered by many to be his best effort, he cleaned up his act, presenting himself in an entirely new light with lots of plans for the future.

Was it perhaps an omen that on the 9th of July, only weeks before his tragic death, a light scaffolding fell on stage destroying the neck of "Number One", his main instrument, a Stratocaster, made of parts from different vintage instruments?

About the solo

It is very difficult to document Stevie Ray Vaughan's guitar style with a single solo. Too many different styles and nuances were combined to form his personal style. As he is mostly influenced by Albert King and Jimi Hendrix, it would be a good idea to try to play the solos in this book from these guitarists á la Stevie Ray Vaughan.

This solo is a 12 bar blues in E and is based on the S.R.V. hit "Pride and Joy". It starts off with an intro and a typically Texan blues rhythm part. This is followed by a solo chorus and finishes off with a nice ending riff. The solo doesn't have any particular problem spots, but the difficulty here is of another kind: aside from trying to sound like Stevie Ray Vaughan., which is an almost impossible task, the key item is, at least in terms of trying to get a similar feeling, to play pretty roughly. Stevie Ray Vaughan had extremely strong, large hands and was not exactly gentle with his guitar.

Besides this, as is so often the case, his equipment played an important role.

Example »47«

Discography: Besides the above mentioned LPs, I particularly recommend the posthumously released: "The sky is crying".

Billy Gibbons
Style Solo

High-Tech Texas-Blues

There are few bands that have stuck together for 25 years in the same line up and at the same time managed, despite this, to continue expanding musically. The Texan band ZZ Top with guitarist Billy Gibbons have done just that. ZZ Top started out as a pure Texas blues trio and had, in 1975, one of the biggest blues hits in recent times with a song titled "Tush". Around the mid 80's the band developed into a more "pop" direction using a lot of pre-programmed drum tracks and synthesizers which brought them, with hits like "Rough Boy" and "Gimme All Your Loving", tremendous commercial success. Since then, ZZ Top have stuck to their fomula for success- a mixture of high-tech keyboards and Texas blues guitar- but demonstrate clearly at every live appearance where their roots lie.

About the solo

This blues brings us back again to the key of A. The rhythm part of the following two choruses connect two simple but very effective Billy Gibbons cliches together with other standard figures. They resemble some of the rhythm guitar patterns from chapter II.

From the standpoint of his solos Billy Gibbons solidly stands in the Texas tradition. His excellent slide playing, however, is more influenced by the Chicago players like Muddy Waters and the other pioneer of electric slide guitar, Elmore James. The second 12 bars of the music are a simple slide solo that is loaded with many classic blues phrases. The note values over the slide symbol in measures 6, 7 and 8 mean that you should slide for the duration of a quarter note on the string indicated in the tablature to the up-coming position. This can also be described as a "portamento".

Discography: On the recently released ZZ Top "Greatest Hits" you'll find a good mixture of this band's most important songs.

Example »48«

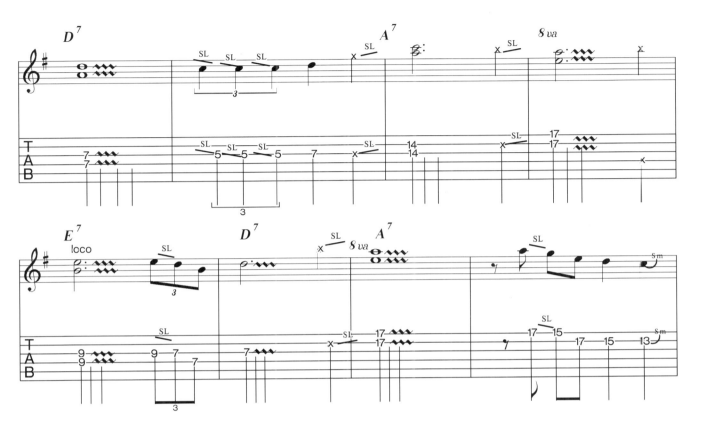

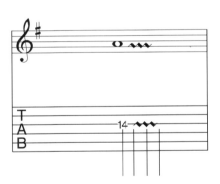

Chapter 9
Fusion Blues

What does the term fusion actually mean? Hmm... good question.

Fusion means a melting together. In the musical sense it means a mixing of different musical styles. Basically fusion is just a hipper version of the term "jazz rock" (which would have done the trick in the first place).

In the middle of the 70's a mixture of jazz influenced harmonies with pop and rock grooves developed on the west coast. The truly new element in this west coast fusion were the guitar improvisations that came out of it such as the playing of Larry Carlton and Robben Ford who had no problems combining rock sound, blues phrasing and knowledge of jazz harmony into a new style.

The blues and the melodic minor scale
The aspect of this style that I find the most interesting is the harmonic one.

Whereas in rock styles the dominant 7th chord is treated mostly with the mixolydian scale, in jazz this is not the case. Here, two modes of the melodic minor scale are often used. These are the fourth (lydian b7 scale: 1 9 3 #11 5 13 b7) and the seventh mode (altered scale: 1 b9 #9 3 b5 #5 b7). These are scales that take a bit of time to get used to as they contain some pretty "outside" sounding notes. So give yourself a chance to get accustomed to the new sounds.

But when can I use these scales?!
The lydian b7 scale, the fourth mode of the melodic minor scale can be used to play over a dominant 7th chord that does not resolve to a tonic (ie. a "static" dominant 7th). For the situation where the dominant 7th does resolve (functional dom.7), regardless of whether you are in a minor or major key, a good scale choice is the seventh mode, the altered scale.
Besides this use, the altered scale, on account of its high tension note content, is often used as a transition to an approaching chord. More information on this subject can be found, by the way, in my book "Rock Guitar Secrets".

What does all this mean for the blues? Here is a blues in A using various "melodic minor" derived scales.

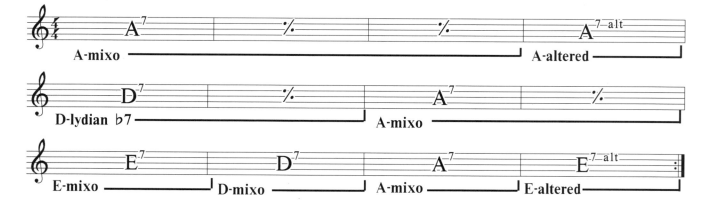

The familiar sound of the mixolydian scale in the first three measures establishes the blues "sound", before the fourth measure introduces tensions by means of the altered scale.

As the subdominant always tends to lead away from the tonic, this effect can be underscored with the use of the lydian ♭7 scale.

If you want to build up the greatest possible tension leading back to the tonic A chord, you can use the E altered scale in the last measure. This playing around with tonal pressures is usually referred to as "tension-resolution".

In the following solos you'll be able to see how these scales sound in context.

Larry Carlton
Style Solo

Mr. 335

Larry Carlton has been, since the early 70's, a time during which he was one of the most sought-after studio players in Los Angeles, one of the driving forces behind the development of modern guitar playing. Besides his solo records, you can also hear his work on LPs from Steely Dan, The Crusaders, Christopher Cross and many others. Legions of other guitarists have tried to imitate his melodic but also harmonically interesting playing. Being able to deliver a "Carlton sound", meaning the combination of a Gibson 335 and a Mesa Boogie amp, is still a must for studio musicians today and he is still refered to as  "Mr. 335" even though he's been playing a different model guitar for 10 years. After many successful years of solo career, he was critically wounded in a robbery and barely survived. Since then he has cut back his activities considerably.

About the solo

The following solo is a 12 bar blues in A. What's interesting here are the chords he uses. They are suspended chords in which the third is replaced by the fourth (described in the chord as an 11th). This sound is much more open than the dominant 7th although the harmonic function is no different. It has the result of giving even simple blues licks a very hip sound. In this sense, you're already holding the "key" to fusion guitar in your hand: colorful chords, blues licks and occasionally a cool jazz line (you can find lots of these, by the way, in chapter XVI). They fit wonderfully into this style. Suspended chords are very typical of fusion and can be found in many fusion tunes.

Here is the chord progression:

What is important for Carlton's style of playing, as well as Robben Fords' is a certain light, loose feeling. Both of these guitarists almost always sound as if they were playing without the slightest effort. You should try to observe this and the unobstructed flow of ideas in their solos as well.

In this solo you'll be able to recognize a number of Carlton's stylistic devices; among others the use of generous portions of breathing room in a manner very similar to B.B. King's.

Measures 4 and 6 are very interesting because of the tension they produce. Here the altered scale and lydian ♭7 scale are called for. The rest of the chords are interpreted with the mixolydian, (but not without the "blues" notes).

Also interesting here is the turnaround. Here Carlton plays away over the 1 which he often does when he wants to signal that he is going to play another chorus.

Robben Ford
Style Solo

Blues Lines

Along with Larry Carlton, Robben Ford is the most important "representative" of west coast fusion guitar. After many years as a sideman for greats such as Jon Mitchell, George Harrison and Miles Davis and as studio guitarist for various acts such as Barry Manilow, KISS and many others Robben Ford returned, with the release of his second solo LP "Talk to your Daughter" in 1988, to his roots: the blues. Although one could hear hints of his loose but dynamic blues style on his very fusion oriented LP "The Inside Story", one definitely noticed the influence of the fusion band, "The Yellowjackets" with which he played. With the release of "Talk to your Daughter" and his latest solo record "Robben Ford and the Blue Line" he has established his reputation as a modern blues guitarist of the highest class.

About the solo

This solo is a very groovy 16 bar minor blues in D. Here is the chord progression:

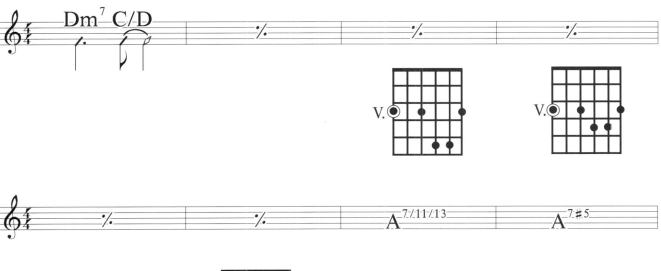

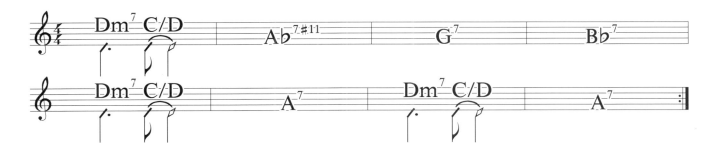

As you can see the changes differ somewhat from a standard minor blues. In this chord progression and the accompanying solo you can once again see the fusion formula that I mentioned while discussing Larry Carlton's colorful harmonies, pop grooves and blues influenced soloing. If you find the solo too difficult, you can simply play the D blues scale over the entire progression. But now let's look at the details; as with the Larry Carlton solo, this solo contains a few very interesting concepts.

The first three measures involve pretty standard blues licks. In measure 4 the Dm[7], C[△7] and Am[7] arpeggios are superimposed over the Dm[7] chord giving the extension notes e, g and ɔ – the 9th, 11th and 13th.
The next cool lick follows in measure 8. Here the altered scale (A altered = Bb mel minor) is used over the altered A[7] chord. Played alongside of all the pentatonic phrases, it really sticks out because of all of its tension notes and gives the solo a certain character. At the end of the solo there is a similar phrase.
When you play your own solos in this style you should try to make a good setting for your hip licks like Robben Ford does by leaving sufficient room between single phrases. This enables the listener to follow the solo better.

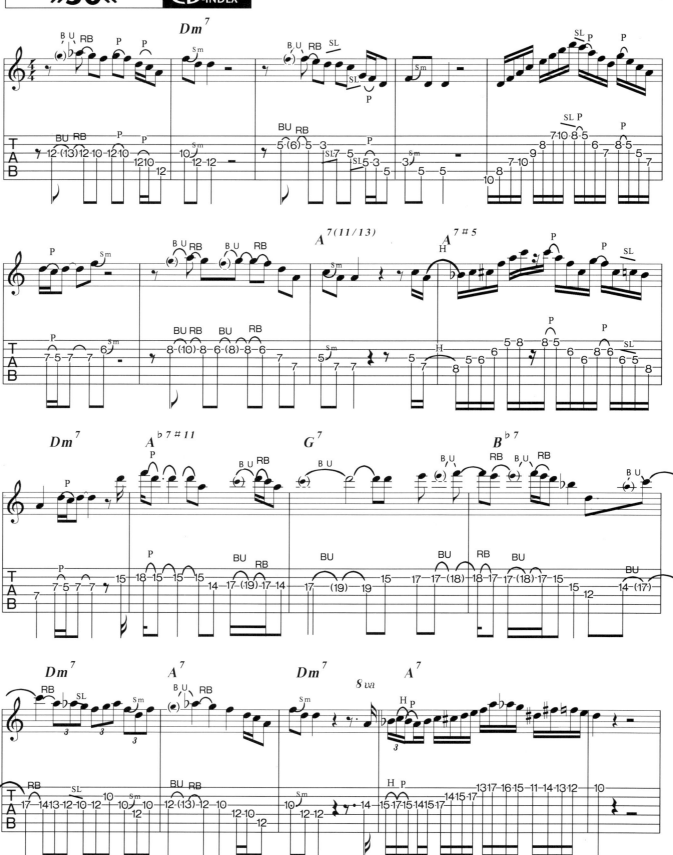

Discography: Listen to the two LPs that I mentioned above.

Chapter 10
Modern Blues Rock

After the late 80's, a period during which the high tech guitar heros (players like Yngwie Malmsteen, Vinnie Moore and others from the neo-classical metal wave and technically oriented guitarists like Steve Vai) ruled, the beginning of the 90's saw a change on the guitar scene: the blues made an unbelievable comeback. Although the techno-trend of the 80's had had the effect of raising the overall technical standard of playing in comparison with that of the previous decade the current direction, with a few exceptions, is towards more feeling, groove and song oriented music. In the guitar playing of hard rock and heavy metal players the enormous success of guitarists like Slash, Nuno Bettencourt and Paul Gilbert steered the trend away from "baroque"-ish sounds and more towards the blues.

Gary Moore
Style Solo

Still Got the Blues

"On the move". This phrase could well be used to describe the constantly changing career of Gary Moore. And the title of his 1990 LP "Still got the Blues" could also be an appropriate subtitle for his musical journey. After 20 years in the music business, Gary Moore returned to his musical roots, where it had all begun for him: the blues. With "Still Got The Blues" and its follow-up album "After Hours", both enriched by guest performances from high-karat blues veterans such as B.B. King, Albert King and Albert Collins, he not only managed to release two excellent modern blues albums and find his true musical identity but also to make the blues acceptable and available to a very wide audience.

About the solo

While the name Gary Moore has been considered for years to be a guarantee of flashy but very emotional rock guitar playing, he has with his two new albums developed his own voice in blues. He pays tribute now and again to established blues greats such as Eric Clapton, Albert King or Paul Gilbert but never without that spark of agressiveness and unpredictability, never sounding like merely a copy of someone else. Besides his "blues on 11" attitude, he has other sides to his musical personality, with unequalled ballads such as "Story of the Blues" or, of course, "Still got the Blues".

The following solo is a combination of both sides. It is a slow, 16 bar minor blues, with a sad melody, that contains many characteristics of Gary Moore's playing. Although this example is not particularily difficult technically, it is important that every note be well-placed.

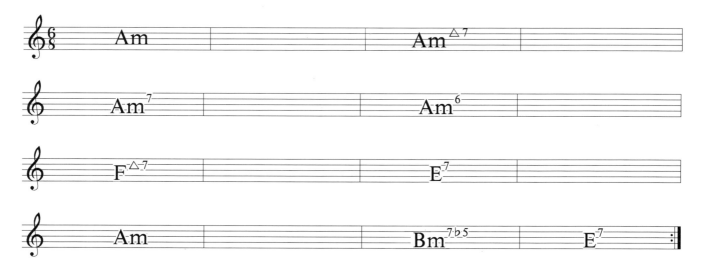

As note material, I primarily use the natural minor scale with added blue notes. Pay attention, as well, to which chord tones the lines resolve to.

What is also interesting is the 6/8 rhythm, which gives a calm feeling to the music.

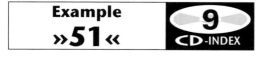

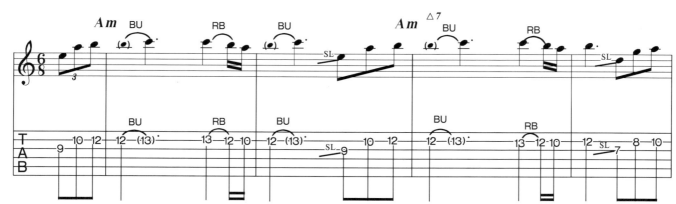

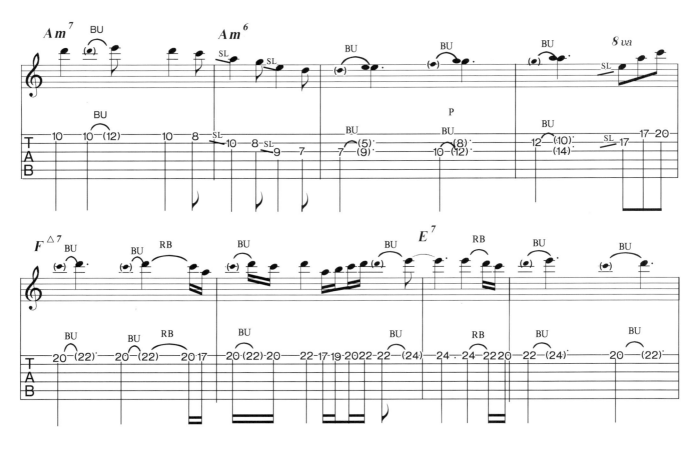

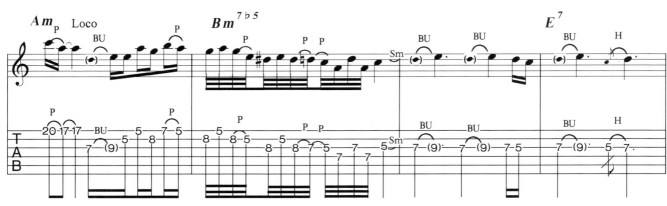

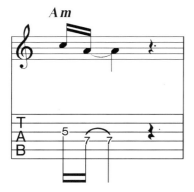

Discography: On the above mentioned albums you can hear a number of interesting grooves and, of course, Gary Moore's blues guitar style.

Modern Blues Metal

The new way of playing the blues

Before you start to work on this solo a word of warning: don't expect to be able to breeze through this solo casually ... it is pretty advanced technically.

It is a 12 bar blues in A, with a very Aerosmith kind of half time groove. Here you should always keep in mind what we discussed in chapter VI, the 16th note triplets as "microtime" (subdivision of the quarter note). From the standpoint of notes I've based this solo on the hip scales also discussed in chapter VI.

The real difficulty comes from the extra 'goodies' that I've built into the lines. In measures 3 and 4 there is a little two-hand lick that is actually not difficult but because of its rhythm doesn't flow so naturally from the fingers. In the 6th measure you'll run into a lick with fifths which is followed in bars 7/8 by some pretty fast string skipping. You should give yourself plenty of time for this lick alone. If you aren't yet accustomed to these techniques I recommend refering to my book "Rock Guitar Secrets" where I give detailed description of these techniques.

The rest of the solo is not really that difficult.

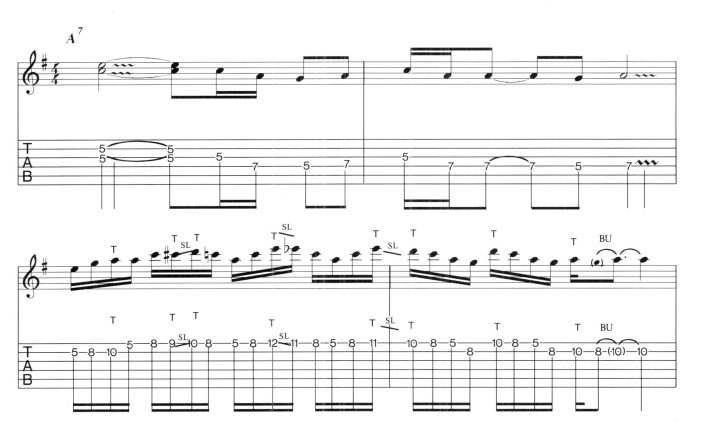

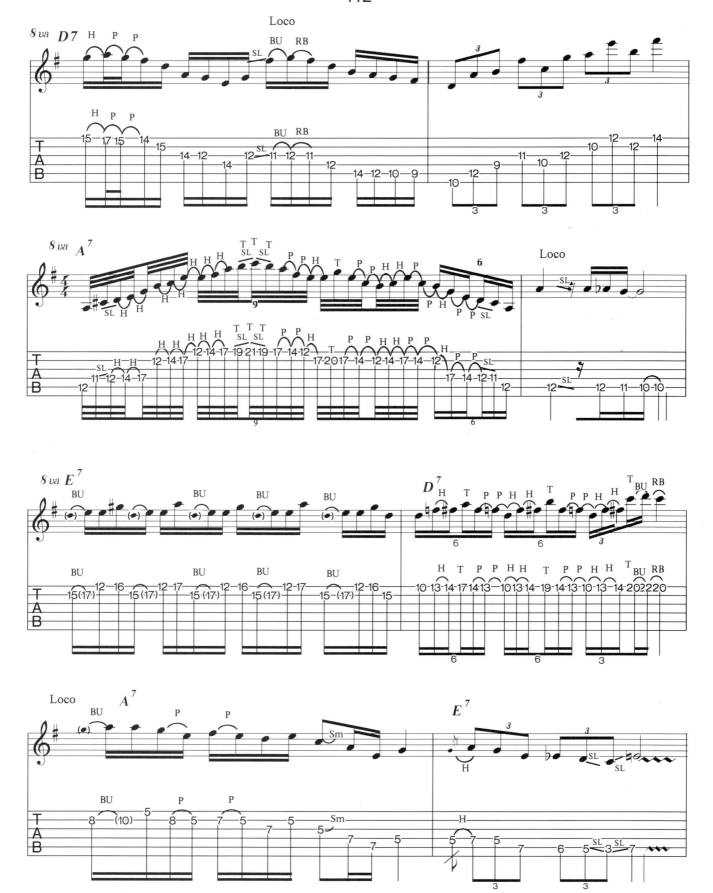

Discography: As an introduction to modern blues metal styles I recommend the following:

Joey Tafolla: "Infrablue"

Michael Lee Firkins: "I"

L.A. Blues Authority (Sampler)

Stage 3

The Jazzblues

After having dealt with various rock oriented interpretations of the conventional 12 bar dominant blues, we'll now look, in stage 3, at some ways in which the blues can be extended using various concepts that come out of jazz.

In jazz blues, just as in traditional blues, there have developed a few standard chord progressons over the years for the dominant, minor and major jazz blues that are common vocabulary and that form the basis for session playing etc. In the following pages you will find various typical chord substitutions as well as the "note material" for improvising over them.

If you find while working with this chapter, that you aren't quite prepared for the material you can get detailed information from my book "Rock Guitar Secrets" to help you fill in the gaps.

Chapter 11
The dominant Jazzblues

In contrast to traditional blues, in jazz blues one hardly finds departures from the 12 bar form such as the 8, 16 or 24 form. This makes things a little bit easier.

Among jazz players the most common version of 12 bar form looks like this.

If you compare this with the standard 12 bar form, you'll notice important differences.

These start in the 8th measure; instead of the usual A^7 you play an $F\#^7$ chord . Originally an $F\#m7$, this chord has developed over the years into a dominant chord in order to provide a stronger "pull" to the following Bm^7.

There is a special description for this situation in music therory. A dominant chord normally leads to a tonic in either major or minor. Now as $F\#^7$ is not the dominant of A^7 (the tonic of the chord progression) but of Bm^7 to which it wants to resolve, $F\#^7$ is called the "secondary dominant" whereas Bm^7 is called temporary tonic.

The next altered part of this blues is the II-V progression in measures 9 and 10: $Bm^7 - E^7$.
The II-V or II-V-I progression plays an extremely central role in jazz harmony. It is derived from the classical cadence I-IV-V (eg. in C major: C major, F major, G major) which has developed into the II-V-I (in C major: Dm^7-G^7-C major 7) that is common today.

The turnaround has changed here as well. Instead of a measure each of A^7 and E^7, we now have a repeat of the last four chords changing twice as quickly as previously.

Just as with traditional blues, there are for this kind of turnaround a great number of possible variations to which I've dedicated chapter XV in this book.

Before we get to the many chord substitutions possible in jazz blues, let's make a little excursion into the subject of jazz improvisation. Now, how and with what material does one jam over this new blues form?

The greatest difficulty will come with the F#7 chord that we looked at in the 8th measure. As it is not a dominant chord that is derived from the mixolydian scale which would resolve to a major chord it resolves to a minor chord.

Possibilities for an appropriate scale here could be
a) B harmonic minor
b) F# altered scale (G melodic minor)
c) F# dominant diminished (G diminished).

I would recommend trying your luck first with the harmonic minor, as it will sound the most familiar to your ears.

You should also play this chord preferably as F#7 and not as F#9, F#11 or F#13.

It is, of course, possible to alter this chord but not without problems. For more information about this, take a look at "chord substitutions" for the dominant jazz blues under the heading "altered chords".

Over the II–V progression that follows in the 8th and 9th measures, you can play the following scales:
over Bm7: B dorian,
over E7   : E mixolydian.

For the turnaround you can use the same scales.

Here is a summary of what we've discussed.

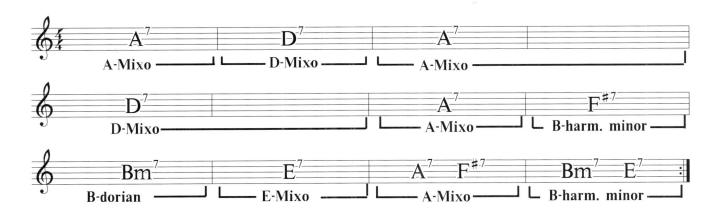

Now here's a "mini jam–track" to get used to the new form and chord–scale choices.

Chord substitutions for the dominant jazz blues.

For this basic form of the dominant jazz blues there are a great variety of harmonic ways of spicing things up to keep it from getting too boring. The basic idea here is to replace a chord or chord progression with other chords without changing the harmonic function. This way you can get very interesting sounds without leaving the musical form of the blues.

As there are often a number of substitution possibilities for certain measures, I've left the measures that are not involved blank, in order to keep things easier to see. With the help of this fairly simple concept you can create an almost unlimited number of different chord progressions.

Substituion 1: the diminished 7th chord.

The first substitution consists of two places in the form where you can substitute a $D\#^{o7}$ for a D^7 chord. How is this possible? The fact responsible for this is that a $D\#^{o7}$ is actually an altered D^7. To be exact it is a $D^{7\flat9}$ with a missing root (or tonic) note.

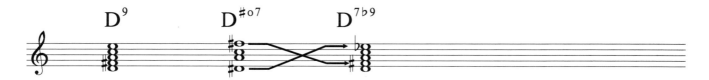

As you see, the $D\#^{o7}$ contains the same notes as $D^{7\flat9}$ only with some notes sitting in a different octave and with enharmonically changed names.

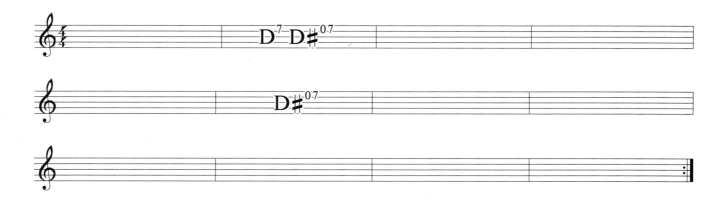

This chord is suitable for two places in the 12 bar form. Remember that the chord $D\#^{o7}$ contains exactly the same tones as $F\#^{o7}$, A^{o7} and C^{o7} and that you can also apply these chords in the same situation.

When improvising over the diminished 7th chord, you can use the diminished scale or diminshed arpeggios.

Substitution 2: The applications of the II–V progression in major and minor

A very popular jazz concept is replacing dominant 7th chords with II–V progressions. The effect produced is that of more motion in the chordal accompaniment, as well as a stronger cadence effect within the blues form. In order to get more variety you can throw these small "jazz" cadences into the form.

For starters there are two places in the blues where they work particularily well:

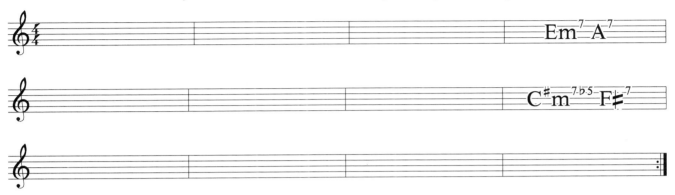

Measure 4: the Em–A^7 leads into the change to D^7.

On top of this progression play, as before, E dorian (Em^7) and A mixolydian (A^7).

Measure 8: C#m^{7b5}–F#^{7} is a II V progression in minor. It has the same function as II–V in major ... intensifying the pull back to the I.

For improvising over C#m^{7b5} play a C# locrian scale (D major scale) and over F#^{7} as mentioned above B harmonic minor.

However, these are not the only places in the blues form where you can substitute the II–V progression. Here are some other possibilities.

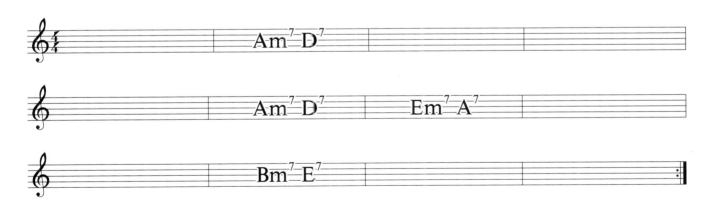

For improvising use the old dorian/mixolydian combination.

By the way, you'll find a couple of hip licks to play over the II–V progression in chapter XVI.

Substitution 3: The altered dominant seventh chord.

Let's talk about jazz! A very important element in jazz is the use of altered dominant seventh chords, in which the already existing tensions of this chord family are further intensified. Particularly effective is the use of these chords when they are a fifth above the chord to which they resolve, in other words when they belong to a V–I progression.

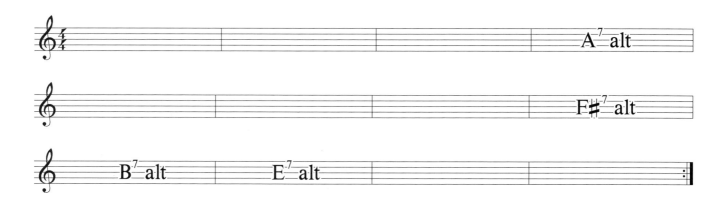

As note material to use for improvising over altered dominants there are a number of scale choices available. Important here is that the alterations of the scale and those of the chord do not conflict with each other. The following scales are appropriate for the above mentioned altered chords:

Whole tone	scale–alterations	♭5, ♯5;
halftone wholetone	scale–alterations	♭5, ♭9, ♯9;
altered	scale–alterations	♭5, ♯5, ♭9, ♯9.

You can, of course, also use these scales in the context of the II–V progression.

Substitution 4: The tritone substitution.

Beside the use of altered chords, there is one very typical "trick" in jazz: the use of the tritone (or ♭5 substitution). The idea behind this term consists of being able to replace any dominant seventh chord with another dominant seventh chord the root of which lies a diminished fifth away.

You'll be able to see this best in a II–V–I progression:

II–V–I in C major: Dm^7–G^7–C major 7.

The G^7 chord is now replaced by $D♭^7$ (G to D♭ is a diminshed fifth). Here the roman numeral chord names change as well:

II–♭II–I in C major: Dm^7–$D♭^7$–C major 7.

This concept is practically omnipresent in jazz. This substitution has the effect of creating a flowing, chromatic downwards motion in the bass from D to C in contrast to the intervallic leaps in the standard II–V–I bass line from G to D to C.

To improvise over this substitution you should use a lydian ♭7 scale, the fourth mode of the harmonic minor (see the chapter on fusion blues). Remember, D♭ lydian ♭7 = A♭ melodic minor.

In our dominant blues, we could theoretically use substitutes of this type for every dominant 7th chord. I would suggest not replacing all of the dominant 7th chords, as this would change to the sound of the blues form too much. Try it first in these parts of the form.

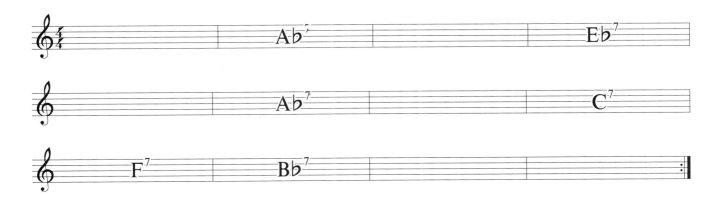

You can also substitute complete II–Vs in major and minor using this technique.

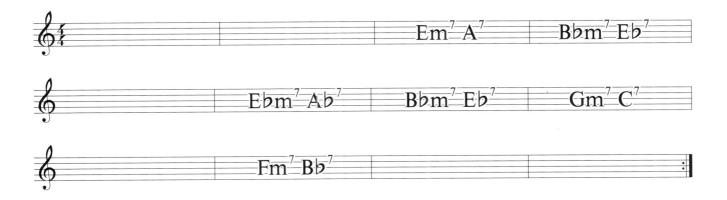

For the purposes of this book, this explanation of tritone substitution should do the trick. There are, however, numerous other ways of using this concept.

Substitution 5: Modal interchange.

As the name suggests this concept involves an interchange of modes in blues. Here you briefly step out of the mixolydian realm and make a short trip through ionian and aeolian territory, then heading back home over the turnaround.

An itinerary for this excursion through the modes might look like this:

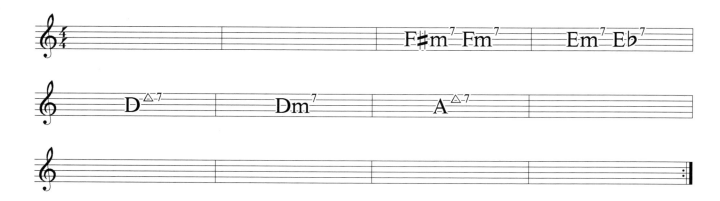

To bring a little more chromatic elements into play, I've taken the original F♯m⁷–Bm⁷–E⁷–A⁷ (III–VI–II–V) that in itself is a common jazzy chord progression and inserted some tritone substitutions. After this there's a substitution of D mixolydian with D ionian (D major 7 instead of D^7). The next chord, Dm^7, is derived from the D minor scale (D aeolian) which, in turn, is resolved to A major 7 (A ionian instead of A mixolydian). Pretty cool, huh? This kind of combination of major and minor is, by the way, a device also found in many pop songs.

Besides the above mentioned modal scales you should also try running F dorian over Fm^7 and E♭ lydian ♭7 over the E♭^{7}.

Chapter 12
The Minor Blues

As with the dominant blues, the minor blues can be "spiced up" as well. Generally speaking, and certainly in terms of concepts and approaches, not much is really different, except for the fact that you're in a minor key.

For the jazz players there is one form of the minor blues which is the basis for the variations which we're about to look at:

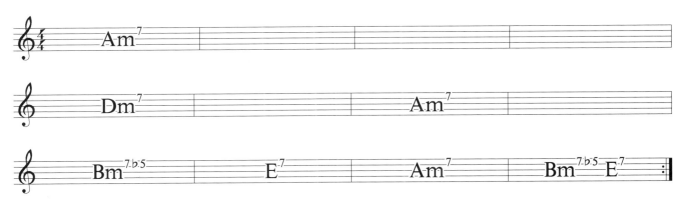

If you compare these changes to those in chapter I, you'll notice right away the addition of two minor II–V progressions (in measures 9/10 and 12). This makes the minor blues sound jazzier already. Playing the rhythm guitar for these changes (as well as the dominant and major blues) in a jazzy way will be described later on in chapter XV. There you'll also find some hip turnarounds for the minor blues. For this reason, I've left the last two measures in the blues in this chapter empty, as I did in the previous chapter.

Chord substitutions for the minor blues.

Substitution 1 The use of II–V's in minor and major.

As in the case of the dominant blues, the II–V progression can be used as a substitute in the minor blues. In the following 12 bar form, you'll find all the better-sounding possibilities for using this device. Remember that you do not, of course, have to use all possible substitutions all of the time. Sometimes one or two is enough to bring a little variety into the form.

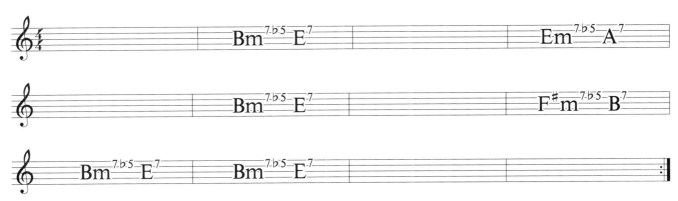

Measures 2, 6 and 9: To get more activity into the form, you can insert a II–V motion in Am into these measures. For improvising, use a B locrian over the Bm⁷ᵇ⁵ (c major) and an E phrygian dominant (A harmonic minor/AHM5) over the E⁷.

Measure 4: Here the change to D minor is led into with a II–V.

Measure 8: Here a II–V in minor resolves to E⁷, which in turn has been replaced by a II–V in A minor.

For jamming the best choice is, once again, the locrian/HM5 combination.

II–V progression in major can also be used in minor blues. This brings more motion into the form and lets the minor blues sound a bit more "major", as paradoxical as this might seem.

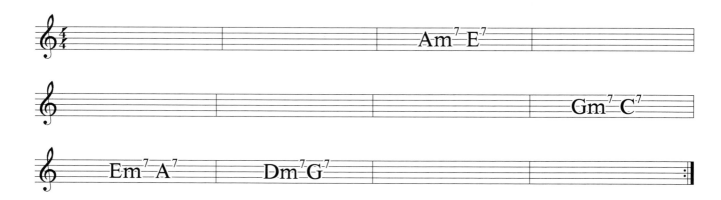

Measure 8: This II–V in F major sounds particularly good when preceded by II–V in A minor.

Measures 9/10: Here we're modulating, for two measures, from Am to C major by inserting the very typical jazz progression III–VI–II–V in C major. In order to add tension to this progression, I've changed the original VI chord, Am, to an A⁷.

Substitution 2: Dominant seventh chords

As with the dominant blues you can also insert dominant sevenths in various places in the minor blues form. The effect of this is similar to the use of the II–V progressions: building a certain amount of tension that is then resolved.

Try out these substitutions.

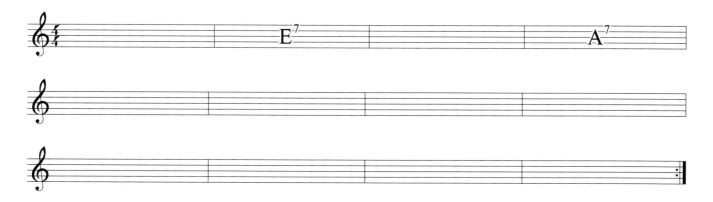

As these dominants are not derived from the mixolydian scale, you should use A harmonic minor over the E⁷ and D harmonic minor over the A⁷ for improvising.

Substitution 3: Altered dominant seventh chords.

To increase the amount of tension of the dominant seventh chords, you can alter them here as well. This works with all dominant seventh chords, regardless of whether they are part of a II–V or just hanging around as single chords.

Besides the already mentioned places where substitution with a dom 7th chord is appropriate, there's also:

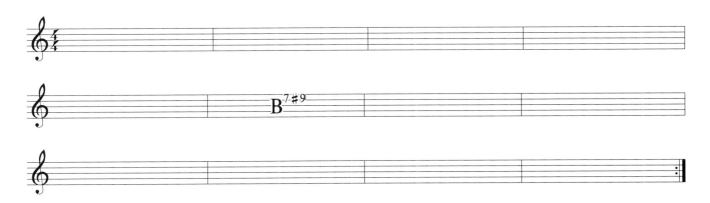

As far as improvising over altered chords, just follow the same rules as with the dominant blues.

Substitution 4: The tritone substitution.

Tritone substitution is governed in the minor blues by the same rules as with the dominant blues. To put it in plainly: jazz makes it work.!

In this chart I've started out by substituting all II–V progressions in minor.

Now we're going to turn to their "colleagues" in major:

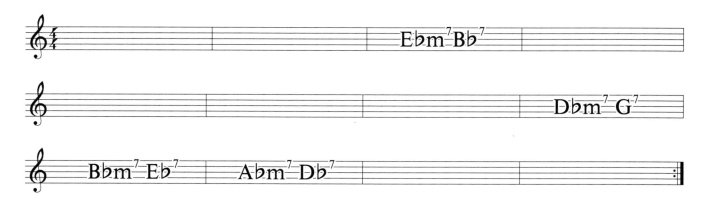

For jamming purposes, once again the dorian/lydian $\flat 7$ works best.
The dominant 7ths shown above, whether they are altered or not, can be also substituted.

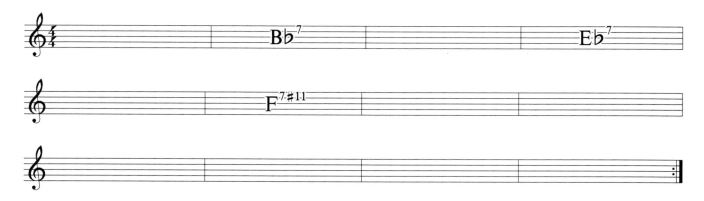

Substitution 5: Major / Minor Chord Relatives

"Major-ish" sounds in a minor blues occur, when major 7th chords are used as substitutes for their relative minor chords. The continuing change between the tonic and subdominant chord which is typical of the major blues also appears in the following diagram. The subdominant chord (Dm^7) is substituted by it's major relative chord (F^{maj7}).
If you would apply this concept to all the other chords you could have the impression of a modulation.

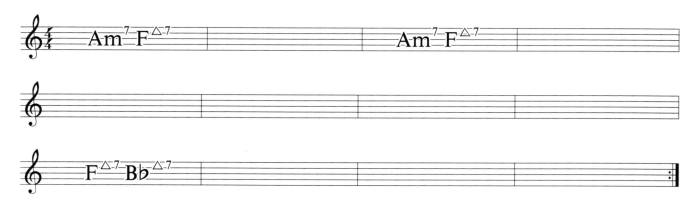

You can improvise over major 7th chords using the same notes as for the minor chord in the same measure, for example the F-lydian scale over a F major 7 chord which represents the A-natural minor scale.

Chapter 13
The Major Jazz Blues

A major blues? Does such a thing exist?

That's actually a good question. Normally the blues is considered to have a melancholy quality and this is certainly true for the most of the blues repertoire. If we look through the great number of songs that are considered to be jazz standards we will find a few that are indeed describable as major blues. They combine blues form and numerous jazzy-sounding major sevenths forming an interesting sounding variant of the blues. A good example of this would be "Blues for Alice" and "Bill's bounce" from **Charlie Parker**.

As a basis for different variations of the major blues, here is a slightly altered version of the dominant blues form in which the dominant seventh chords are replaced by major sevenths.

An alternative to this form is one in which the A major 7 in measure 7 is replaced by C#m^7 ... a very common diatonic substitution, by the way.

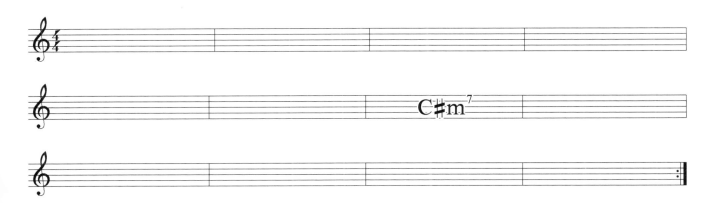

As all the chords here are diatonic, chords in the key of A major(i.e. built out of scale notes), it is pretty easy to jam on these changes: A major fits perfectly.

Chord substitutions for the major blues

Substitution 1: Use of the II-V progression in major and minor

As in the dominant and minor blues, there are a number of places in the major blues where we can insert II-V progressions. The effect is the same ... it brings more movement into the blues form. But as we've already said it isn't necessarily hip to play everything you know in one chorus. Be tasty, dude!

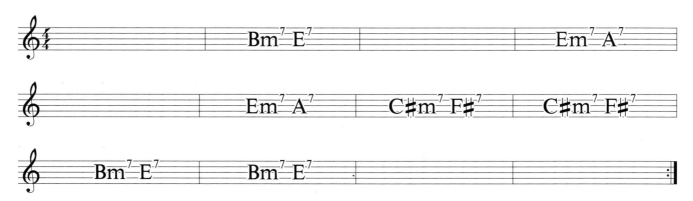

As scale material the by-now-familiar combination of dorian/mixolydian works best.

This variant sounds as if it modulates.

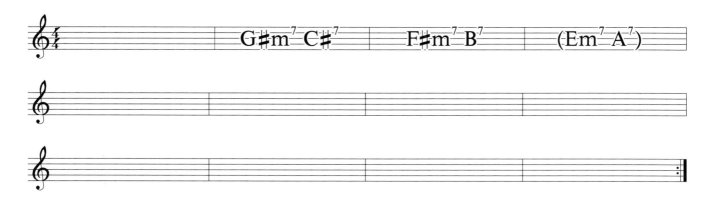

A II-V in minor in the same spot sounds very exciting.

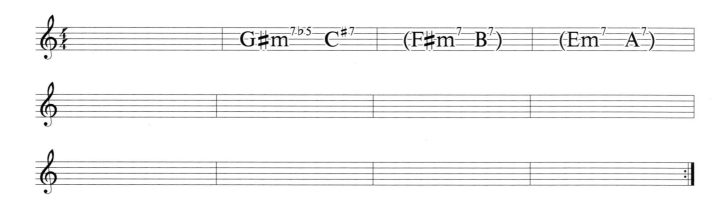

Substitution 2: Modal interchange

You can use the concept of modal interchange in the major blues as well. The IV chord becomes, as before, a minor chord.

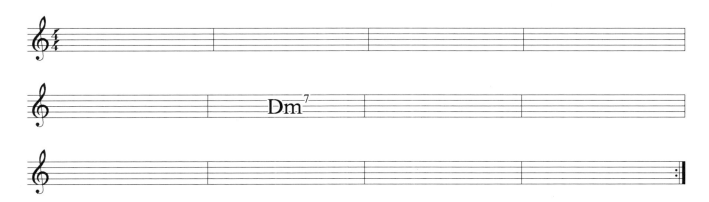

After this modulation, it is common to find II–V's descending in half steps. At high tempos this sounds very "be-bop"-ish.

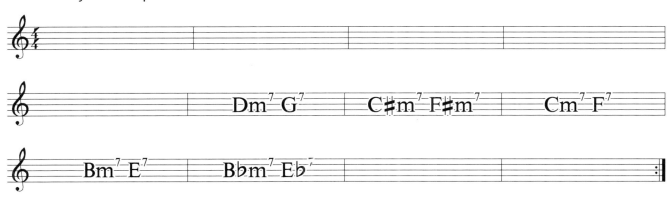

Of course, you can alter all of the dominant 7th chords in the preceding examples.

Substitution 3: The tritone substitution

You can get very chromatic by replacing the V's of the II–V progressions with the tritone substitution. To intensify this effect I've altered all the dom 7ths somewhat.

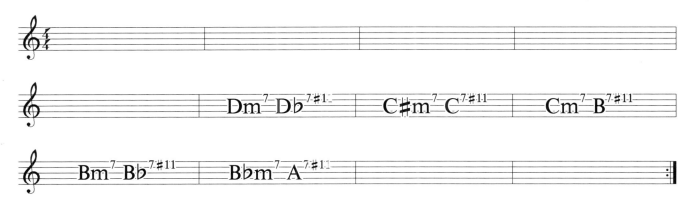

To jam over this chord progression play the respective lydian $\flat 7$ scale of each chord.

Chapter 14 Jazzblues Comping

As with "normal" blues, in jazz blues there are a number of typical accompanying patterns that, although relatively simple, sound very authentic.

1–3–7 voicings

As you may have noticed in the previous chapter, the chords used are often altered or one can use different scales over one chord depending on the alterations in the chord. It is important for this reason, in my opinion, to keep the chord accompaniment relatively neutral until the turnaround. That means reducing the chord to its most important notes. These notes are the root, third and seventh. If you stick to these three notes while comping, the solo voice, whether it is a singer or an instrument, will have quite a bit of freedom and room to experiment with alterations without colliding into your chords. Besides, this will also make strongly colored turnarounds (chapter XV) more effective.

Here are some chord voicings. They contain only the three important notes and are therefore quite easy to play.

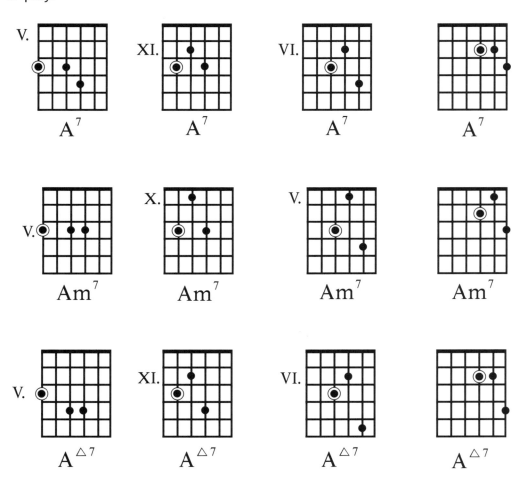

 Attention: don't play any notes but the fretted ones!

With these voicings you can play all the variations on the blues presented in this book. Of course, you can also use other voicings that you already know, but, as we've said, you'll have to pay attention to the alterations. Insteac of a minor 7♭5 chord, which often turns up in a minor blues, simply play one of the above mentioned minor chords.

The rhythm is also very simple. Every quarter note becomes a chordal stroke. This sounds best when you strike the strings with the flesh of your thumb. This rhythm pattern may seem to you a bit of a cliche but watch out! ... gettirg these quarter notes to swing is not easy.

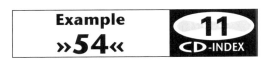

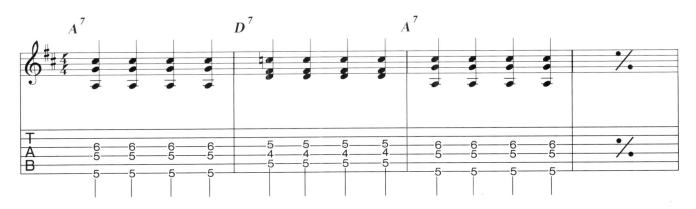

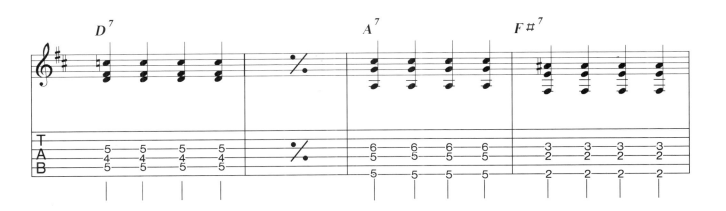

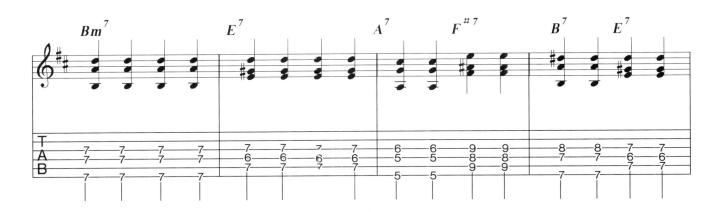

Dominant 7th chords sound particularly good if you hammer-on the major third. For this, it is better if you pick all the notes of the chord.

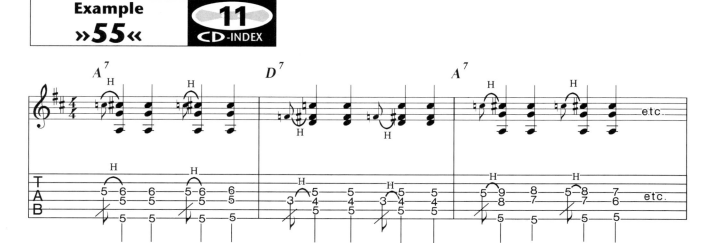

By the way, try playing the rhythm in example 12 (p. 27) using this technique.

Project:

Play all the blues forms like this. Try using as many different voicings as possible.

To sound even jazzier, slide into the chord chromatically from below or above. The resulting harmonies sound pretty hip and are, for guitarists, quite easy to play.

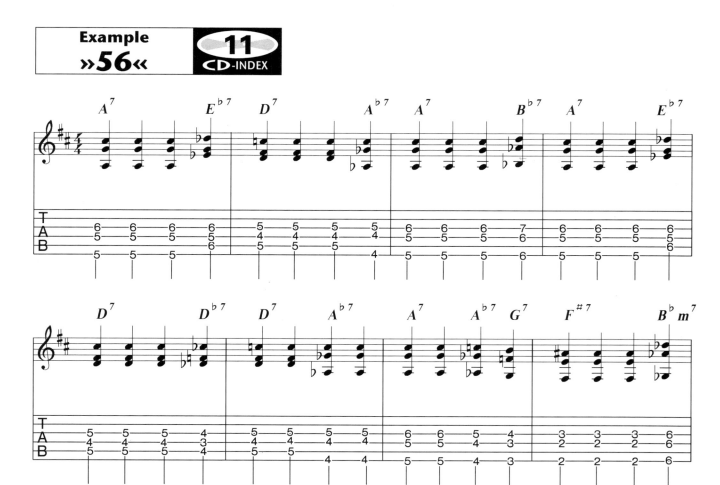

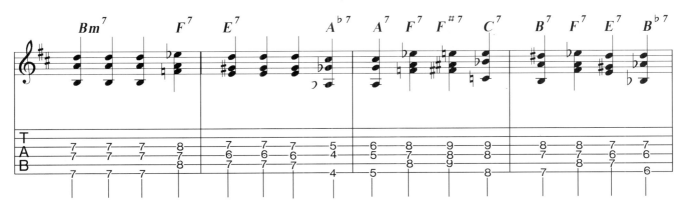

Walking bass lines

A very typical style of jazz rhythm guitar is the playing of walking bass lines. By this I mean simultaneously playing a quarter note bass melody and a chord accompaniment. This is especially useful in musical situations where the guitar has a lot of "room" to work in (such as a duo, for example).

This sounds very difficult, but you'll soon see that it's easier than it sounds. By the way a good listening suggestion for this way of playing jazz blues is Joe Pass.

The first step is to compose a bass melody. A good starting point would be the chromatic motion in the previous example. Here is a bass line based on those changes.

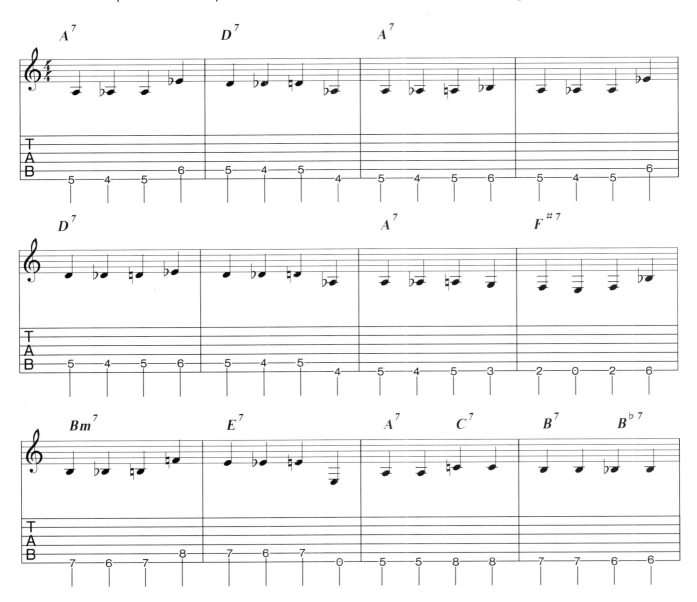

Now play the upper notes, the 1–3–7 voicings that we recently looked at, thrown in between the bass notes.

From the standpoint of technique a very practical way to play this style is with the fingers: the bass is played with the thumb and the chords are plucked with the finger. So in order not to have to put down the pick (or glue it to my forehead with spit) I solve the problem like this:

This bass melody is somewhat more difficult. It is more arpeggio based, ie. the chord tones are used as target notes and chromatic passing notes are inserted in between them. To keep this from getting too difficult, I've avoided to use the additional chords above the bass melody too often.

Has it occurred to you that the fill-in chords mostly are only moved in half-steps?

Project:

Break up the example above into one or several measure fragments and put them in a different order.

Make your own melodies and fragments.

You can also play minor and major jazz blues progressions in this manner.

Blues comping fragments

The next step could be the harmonizations of the bass melodies. Here are a few one measure fragments that you can combine as you like. You can use them (like building blocks) to put together a blues accompaniment. If these small movements are too fast for you, you can also play them as two bar patterns, playing every chord twice as long.

Here are three dominant fragments. Fragments 1 and 2 are, on account of their deep register, particularly well suited for playing in situations without a keyboard.

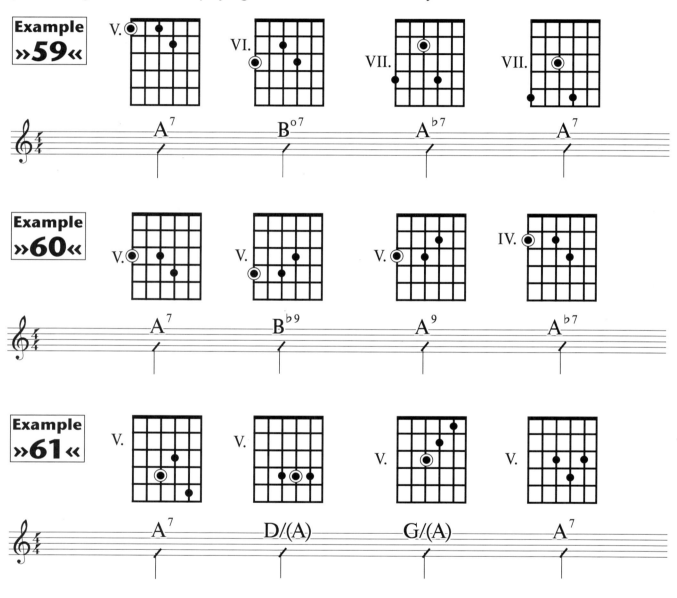

The following minor fragments have more of a dorian sound.

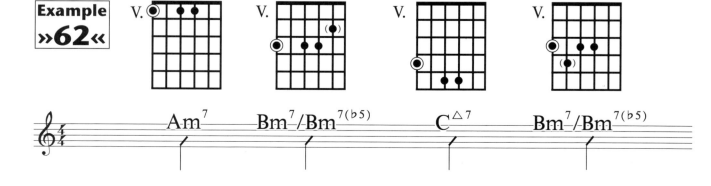

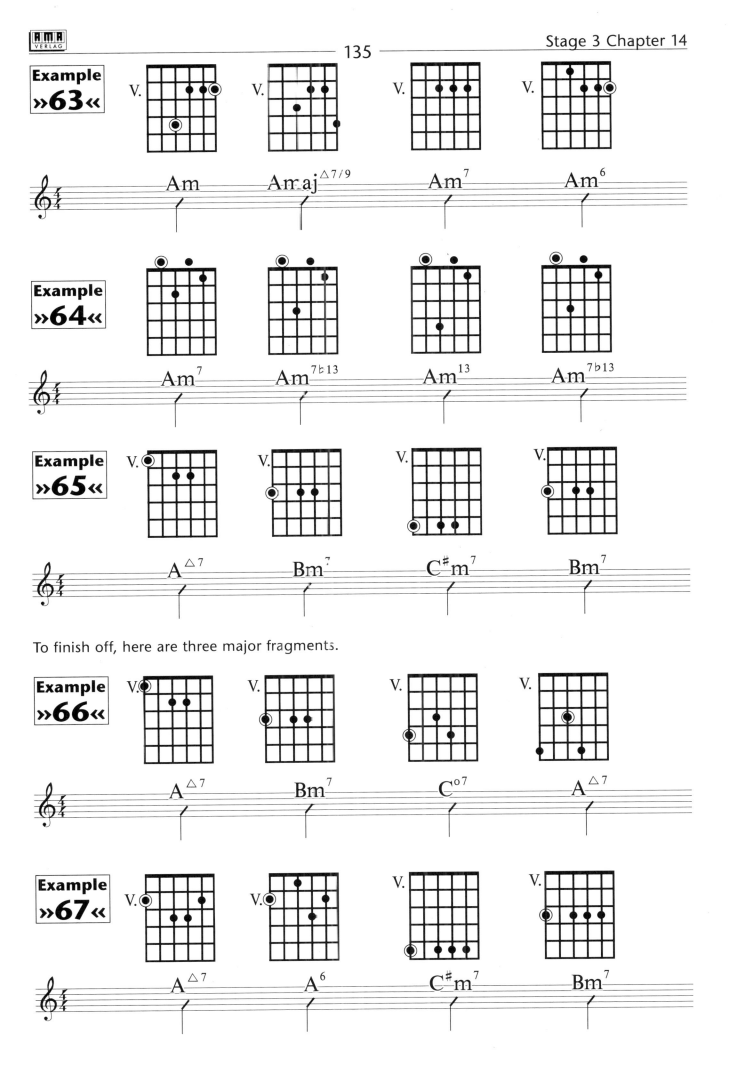

To finish off, here are three major fragments.

Here is an example:

Example »68«

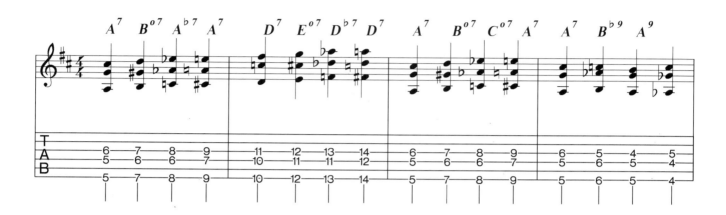

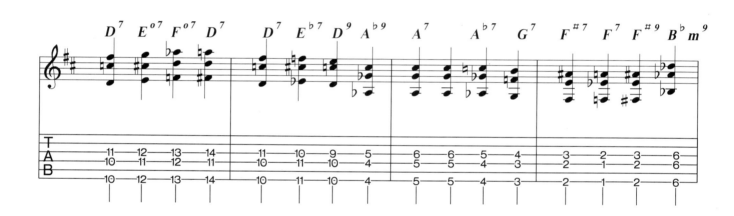

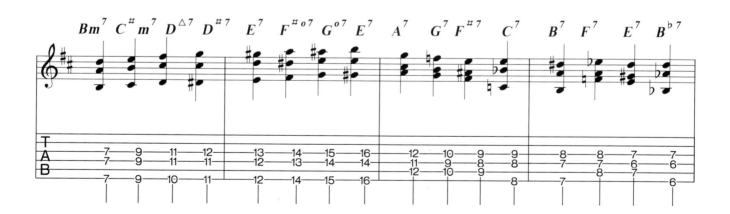

Project:

Play the above mentioned fragment on other strings. Invent your own fragments.

Chord scales

Another hip way to comp is with chord scales. This is a concept that comes from chord melody playing. The idea behind it is really quite simple. Here is an A mixolydian scale:

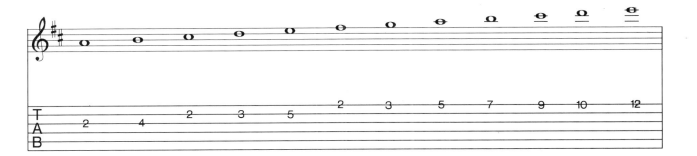

Next, we add an A^7 chord to every note in the scale. To give more color, I've alternated between A^7 and $A^{9\,sus4}$ (commonly known as A^{11} or A^{sus}).

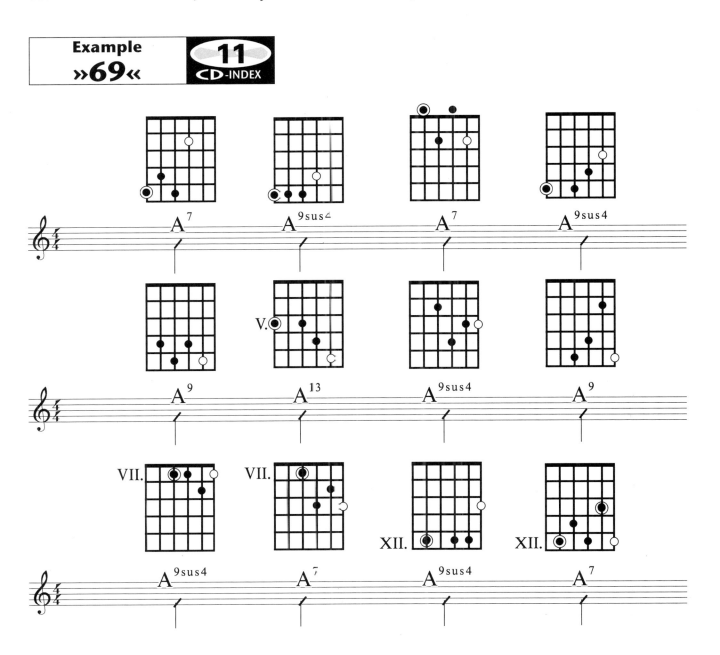

Chromatic notes as well can be played in this way using diminshed 7th chords.
A mixolydian with chromatic passing tones:

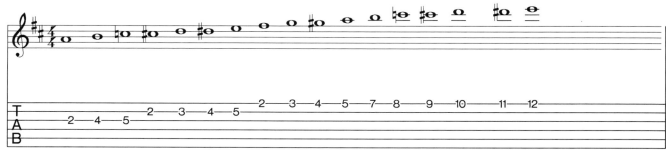

Example
»70«

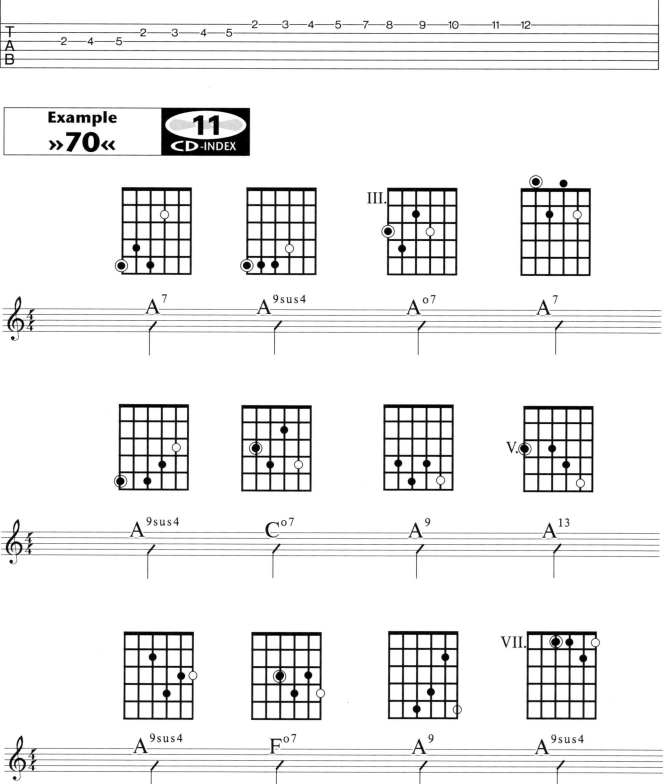

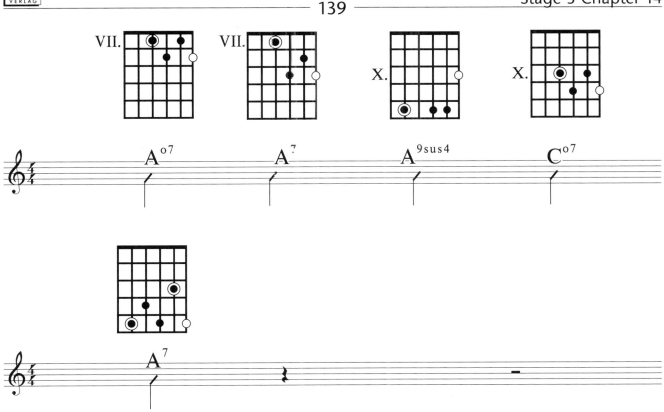

With the help of this technique you can now compose countless comping melodies and fragments. All you have to do is simply find 3 or 4 notes, add the right chords and some rhythm and you're ready to go! This procedure can also be very hip used in other styles like pop or fusion.

Here's an example:

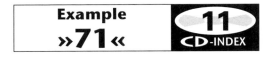

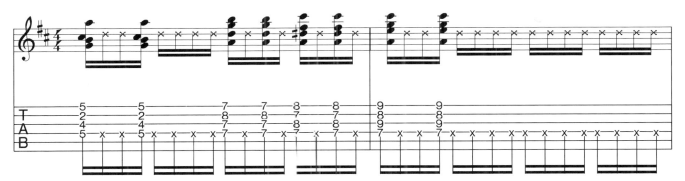

Project:

You can probably guess ... you got it!

Apply the above mentioned principle to the dorian and aeolian scales for minor chords, as well as the ionian and the lydian (for the IV chord) modes.

II–V–I progressions

As a final comping idea, we now come to a few variations on playing II–V–I progressons with interesting voicings. As the majority of jazz standards are loaded with these progressions, you'll find that this material comes in handy.

The following examples are all in C major or A minor. Some of the voicings are pretty dissonant and open, but try to work them, somehow, into your chordal vocabulary.

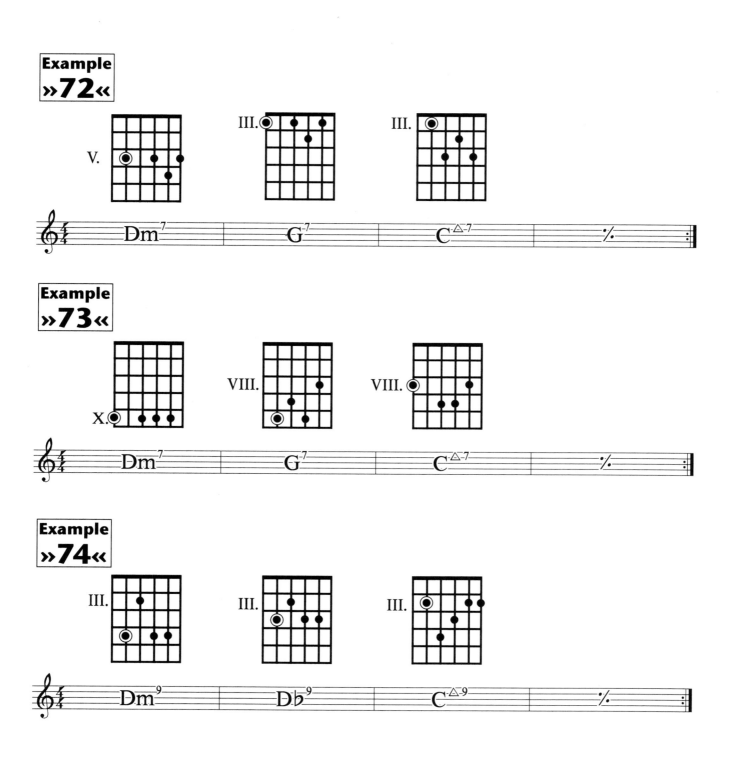

Example »75«

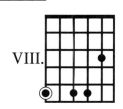 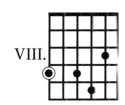 

Dm^{11} $Db^{7\#11}$ $C^{-\triangle 9}$

Example »76«

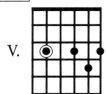  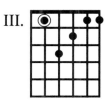

Dm^{7} $G^{-13 b9}$ $C^{-\triangle 9}$

Example »77«

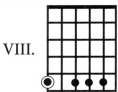 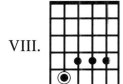 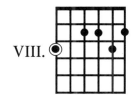

Dm^{7} $G^{-13 b9}$ $C^{-\triangle 13}$

Example »78«

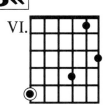 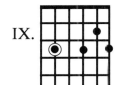 

Dm^{9} $G^{-7 b9}$ $C^{-\triangle 7}$

BLUES
GUITAR
RULES

142

AMA
VERLAG

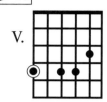

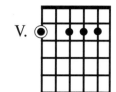

Example
»79«

V.   V.   V.

$Bm^{7\cdot\flat5}$ $E^{7\cdot\flat9}$ Am^{7}

Example
»80«

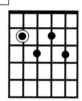

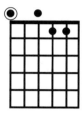

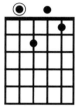

$Bm^{7\cdot\flat5}$ $E^{7\cdot\sharp5}$ Am^{7}

Example
»81«

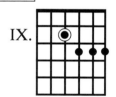

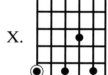

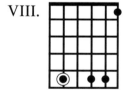

IX.   X.   VIII.

$Bm^{7\cdot\flat5}$ $E^{7\cdot\flat9}$ Am^{9}

Example
»82«

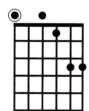

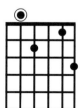

$Bm^{7\cdot\flat5}$ $E^{7\cdot\sharp9}$ Am^{7}

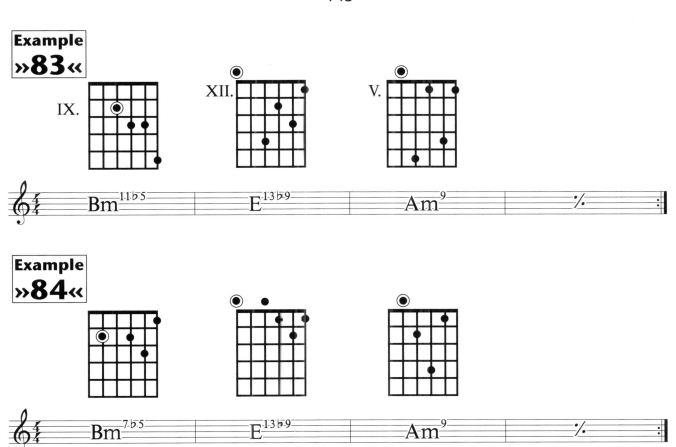

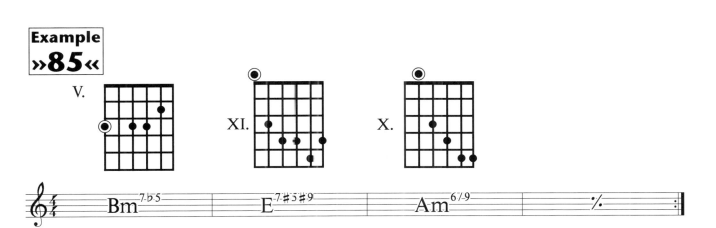

Chapter 15
Turnarounds

Just as in the rock oriented blues the turnaround in jazz blues is a kind of "feature spot" in which the rhythm section as well as the soloist can show what they've got up their sleeve harmonically. I've already demonstrated this in blues rock in chapter III. The following pages contain a number of turnarounds for various kinds of jazz blues. Some of them involve dissonances that you may need some time to get used to. But who ever said that music was all smooth sailing?! I've left the rhythms on the following turnarounds pretty simple. Feel free to change them as you like.

Turnarounds for the dominant blues

As a starting point for the dominant blues turnaround I'll use the following two measures:

This two–chord–per–measure progression contains exactly the four chords as the four preceding measures, but played twice as fast (compare with chapter XII).
To improvise over them you can also use the scales that we've recommended in the above mentioned chapter.

Over	A^7	:	A mixolydian	(D major),
	$F\#^7$	:	F♯ phrygian dominant	(B harmonic minor),
	Bm^7	:	B dorian	(A major),
	E^7	:	E mixolydian	(A major).

Besides the II–V–I progression, this is a very common progression in both jazz and pop music. It is called, in functional harmony, the I–VI–II–V. You should practice jamming over this progression until you can get through the changes with little effort.

In the event that you find the chord changes in the turnaround too quick, I'd advise you to play them with more space between them (for example a new chord every two measures) when recording and then to improvise over them.

Turnaround 1

To get more blues into this turnaround you can make the Bm^7 a dom 7th which leads you to the first turnaround. Over B^7 you can play the B mixolydian.

Here is one way to play this turnaround.

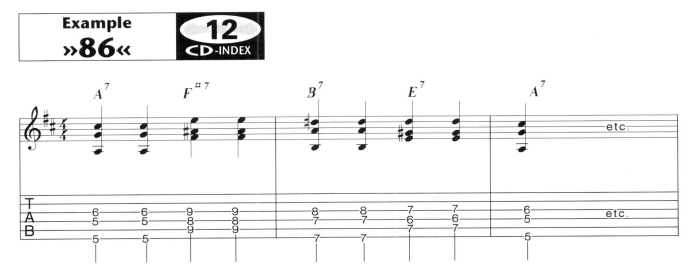

These voicings, consisting of only the root, third and seventh are easy to play and sound good. As the intervals on the D and G string remain the same and are merely slid up and down the fingerboard, the chord changes sound very fluid.

Turnaround 2

This effect is intensified when you add another note. The dissonance increases as well.
As the E^7 chord is now altered, I recommend using the altered scale over it.

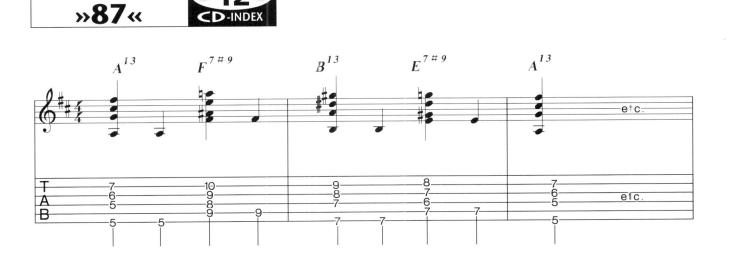

Turnaround 3

Here I've substituted every second chord from the first turnaround with a tritone substitution. This produces a very jazzy-sounding chromatic bass line.

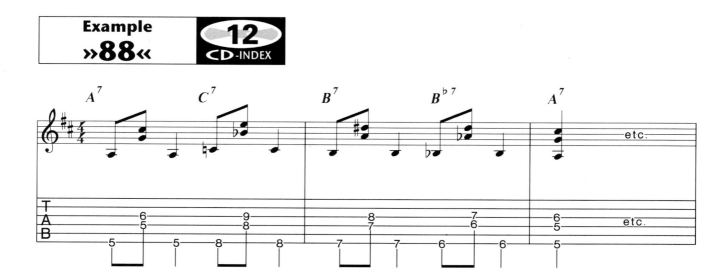

As always with the ♭5 subs, use the respective lydian ♭7 scale.

Turnaround 4

This turnaround has a strong "walking bass", feel to it. You can also find a couple of bII subs.

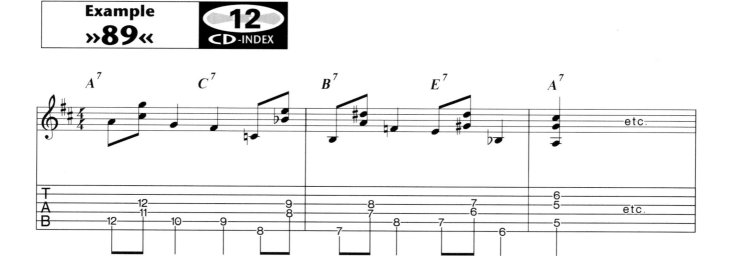

Turnaround 5

Another very popular device in rhythm guitar is the use of common tones. The concept here is to keep a particular tone sounding through all the chords in the progression. Depending on the note, and the respective chords this can be either a chord tone, a chordal extension or an alteration.

In this example, I've added the note F♯ to the original turnaround chords. In the A^7 this note is a 13th, in the $F♯^7$ it is the root, in the B^7 it is the fifth and in the E^7 the 9th. The effect on the ear is to make the impression of very tight voice leading, and that the individual chords are well connected with one another.

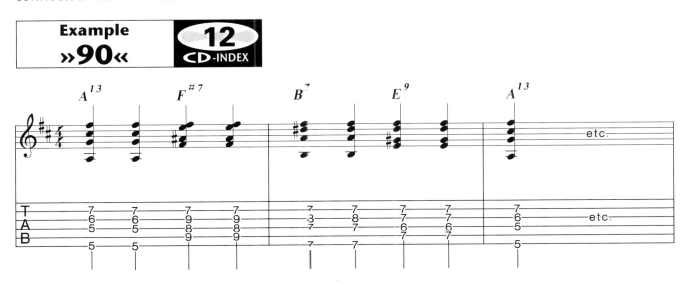

Turnaround 6

In this turnaround the common tone is the note G. It gives this example a more dissonant sound. The G makes the $F♯^7$ into an $F♯^{7♭9}$, the B^7 into a $B^{7♯5}$ and the E^7 into an $E^{7♯9}$.

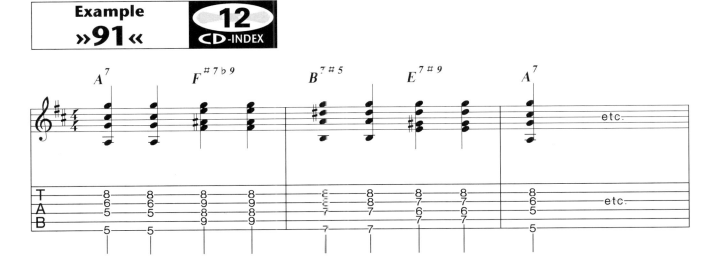

You can use a wholetone scale over $B^{7♯5}$.

Turnarounds for the minor jazz blues.

For the following turnarounds our basic progression will be:

Here the situation is similar to that of the dominant jazz blues. The last two measures have exactly the same progression as the preceding four measures but they are played twice as fast. For improvisation, use these scales:

over Am	:	A dorian	(G major) or A aeloian (C major),
Bm^{7b5}	:	B locrian	(C major),
E^7	:	E phrygian dominant	(A harmonic minor).

Turnaround 1

To give the Am chord a little more pep, you can add a major 7th to it.

Over A minor major 7th you can play either the melodic or harmonic minor scale.

Turnaround 2

The major/minor chord relatives work quite well in the turnaround. An explanation of this term can be found in chapter XIII.

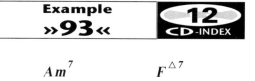

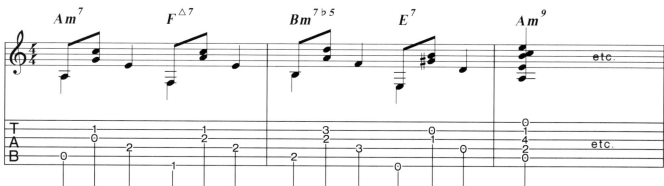

Turnaround 3

In the following example, I've used both the tritone substitution and the common tone concept.

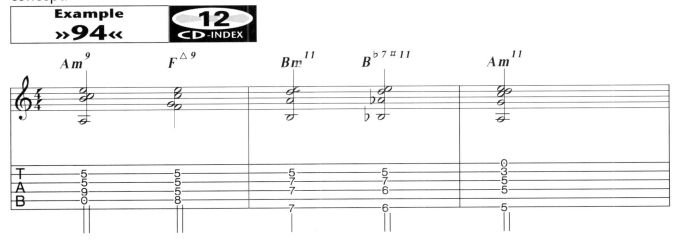

To play over the Bb$^{7\#11}$, use the Bb lydian dominant scale.

Turnaround 4

In this variation I've built in a little melodic movement. These chords are "fingerbusters" from my first book "Chords that hurt" (Tendonitis publishers).

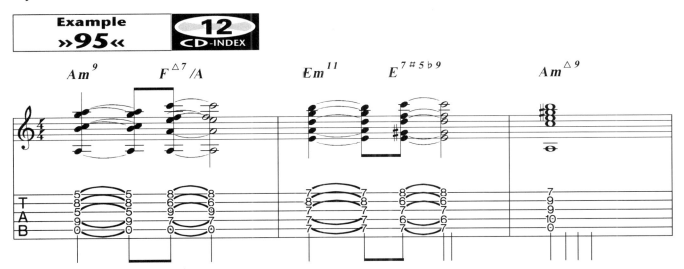

Turnaround 5

In this turnaround I've combined the tritone sub with a bass line.

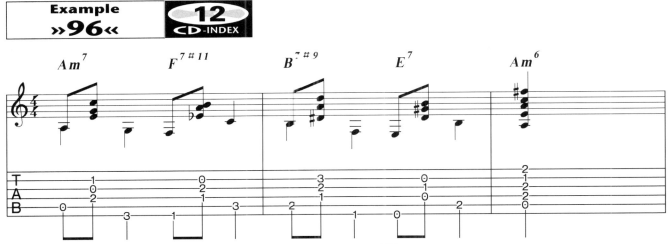

On the F$^{\#11}$ play an F lydian dominant and over the B$^{7\#9}$ a B altered scale. Have fun!

Turnaround 6

This turnaround has a very chromatic bass line.
Particularly interesting here is that in this variation a major 7♯11 and a dominant 7♯11 with the same root occur pretty close to one another in the progression. Note the little melody, as well, in the top voice.

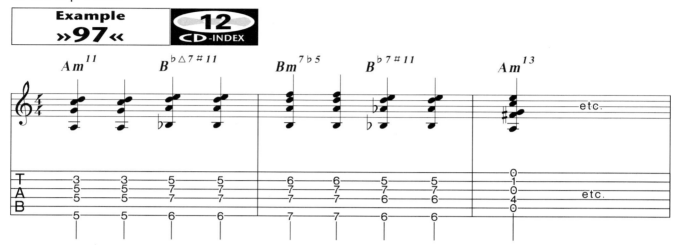

Over Bb△7♯11 you can play Bb lydian (F major) scale, over Bb7♯11 a Bb lydian dominant (F melodic minor).

Turnarounds for the major jazz blues.

There are also some pretty good sounding turnarounds for the major jazz blues. As the tonal differences between the major and dominant turnarounds is not so great in comparison to the minor variations, you can use the following examples in dominant blues as well.
As a basis for the following examples we will be using this chord progression:

As all these chords are diatonic chords out of A major. You can use this scale as improvisational material over them.

Turnaround 1

This first variation again uses the mixture of tritone substitution and the common tone principle ... plus a high count of chromatics.

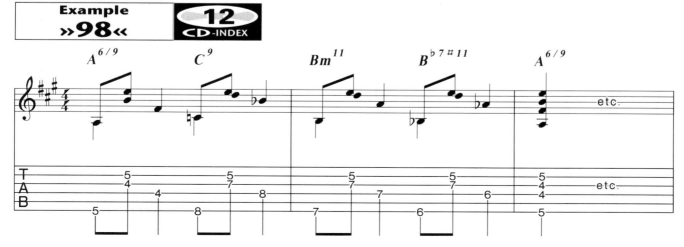

Turnaround 2

In this turnaround a major triad is moved downwards chromatically while the bass notes change normally. The result is a good portion of dissonance. In addition A major 7 is replaced by C#m7.

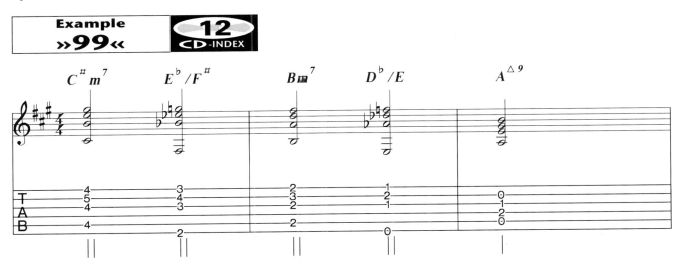

Over both dom 13b9 chords, play their respective halftone–wholetone scales (or more simply said, the diminished scale half a step higher).

Turnaround 3

This variation is similar.

Over both of the altered chords, the best choice is the HTWT scale.

Turnaround 4

Here the chords change somewhat more rapidly.

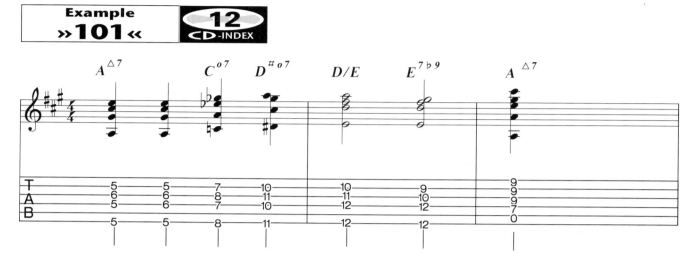

As both the diminshed chords here contain exactly the same as A^0 and $F\#^0$, you cn play one scale over them: A (or C, or D♯, or F♯) diminished.

Turnarounds 5 and 6

The next two variations are a little bit chord melody oriented. They are particularly effective when used as intros.

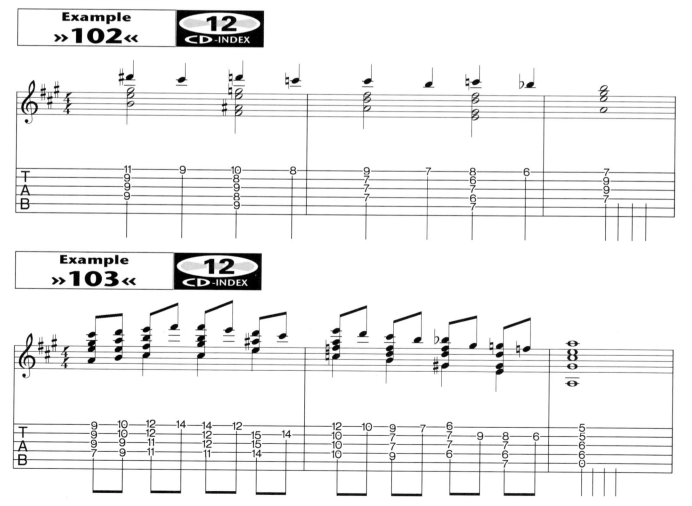

In the next chapter there'll be lots of really hip licks for playing over tricky harmonic situations.

Chapter 16
Jazzblues Licks and Lines

So now we get into the good stuff! In stage 1 and 2 of this book, I've gone pretty much into detail about different improvisational concepts for the blues. These apply to the jazz blues as well. What we looked at in terms of improvisational structure, (A–A–B structure, etc) ... it all still holds. The big obstacles to fluent improvisation over the dominant blues are, in my opinion, the little harmonic pitfalls, such as II–V progressions, secondary dominants and turnarounds. The following section deals with these difficult situations. In many areas learning music is quite similar to learning language. And just as in learning a foreign language it is always a good idea to have a few special phrases in store which help in certain situations. For example, such critical items as "Yesterday at the dentist's" or "Lately at the Hairstylist's" for occasions where one has to know just the right expression.

It is also a good idea to have a few appropriate licks to play over the harmonically difficult parts of the jazz blues.

Licks for the II–V–I progression

In the course of the third section of "Blues Guitar Rules", we've covered almost all the common scale material that can be used to jam over the different chords. Now we'll look at a few licks where this information is put into practice, together with a short harmonic analysis. All licks are intended to be played with a swing feel.

II–V–I licks in major

The following licks all work over a II–V–I progression in C major, Dm^7, G^7, C^{maj7} or their extension.

Lick 1

The interesting thing about this lick is the E major triad over G^7 in bar 2.

Dm^7	:	D-dorian with chromatic passing tones
G^7	:	E-maj triad (G^{13b9} sound)
C$^{\triangle 7}$	:	C-ionian

Example »104« **13 CD-INDEX**

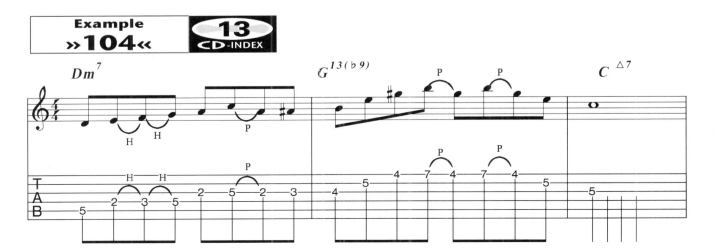

Lick 2

This phrase sounds best if you play Db^7 (the $b5$ substitution) instead of G^7.

Dm^7	:	D-dorian
G^7	:	D^b major triad
$C^{\triangle 7}$	:	C-ionian

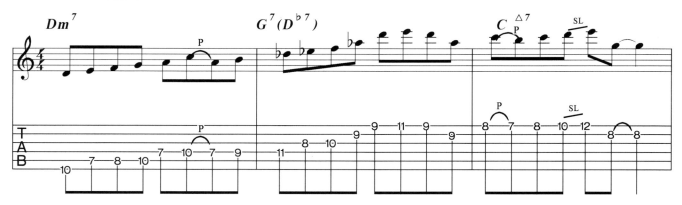

Lick 3

With these licks, arpeggios come into play.

Dm^7	:	$Dm^{7\ arp}$
G^7	:	B diminished scale
$C^{\triangle 7}$	:	C-ionian with chromatic notes

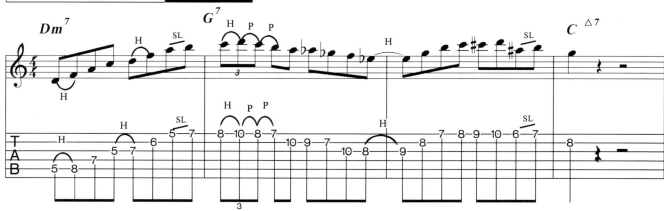

Lick 4

Dm^7	:	F^{maj7} arp
G^7	:	B altered (a^b mel. minor)
C^{maj7}	:	C-ionian with chromatic notes

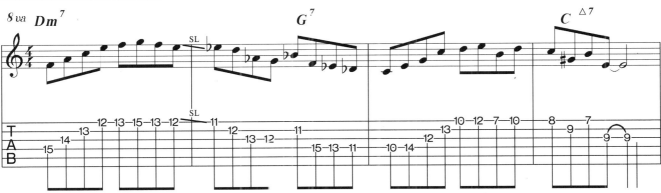

Lick 5

Now we're gonna get chromatic!

Dm^7	:	D-dorian with chromatics
G^7	:	G-altered with chromatics
C^{maj7}	:	C-ionian with chromatics

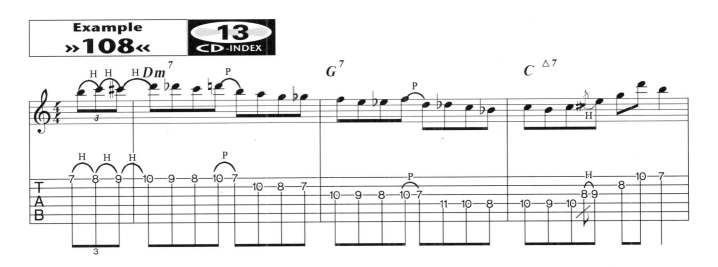

These licks sound pretty cool if you use them á la George Benson over a Dm^7 funk vamp. As the V chord is mostly altered within the II–V–I licks, this produces interesting tensions. The static quality of a one-chord vamp (an accompaniment for improvisation using only one harmony) as in this example, is broken up in this way.

II–V–I licks in minor

Lick 1

As in many II–V–I progressions, here the harmonic minor scale is used.

Bm^{7b5}	:	Bm^{7b5} arp
E^7	:	A harmonic minor
Am^7	:	A harmonic minor

Example »110« CD-INDEX 13

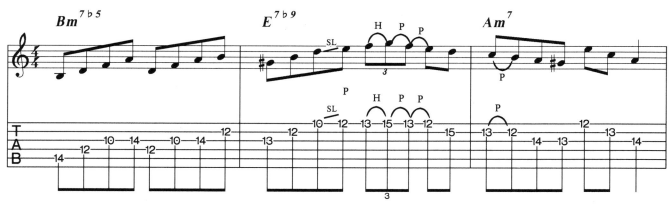

Lick 2

This lick combines various concepts.

Bm^{7b5}	:	B-locrian nat. 2 (D mel. minor)
E^7	:	augmented triads on G♯ and C
Am	:	Am^7 and Em^7 arp

Example »111« CD-INDEX 13

Lick 3

Here, once again, harmonic minor rules!

Bm⁷ᵇ⁵	:	B-locrian with chromatics

Bm^{7b5} : B-locrian with chromatics

E^7 : A-harmonic minor

Am^7 : A-aeolian

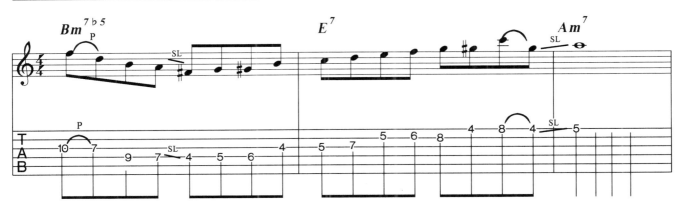

Lick4

Bm^{7b5} : A-harmonic minor

E^7 : A-harmonic minor

Am^7 : A-melodic minor and A-dorian

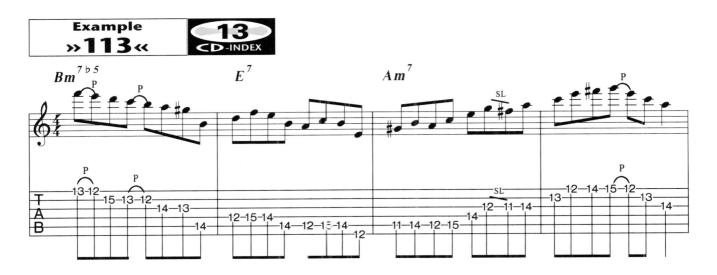

Lick 5

Here is a lick with arps.

Bm^{7b5} : $D^{\triangle 9}$ arp

E^7 : $F^{\triangle 7}$ arp

Am^7 : A-dorian

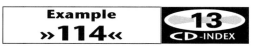

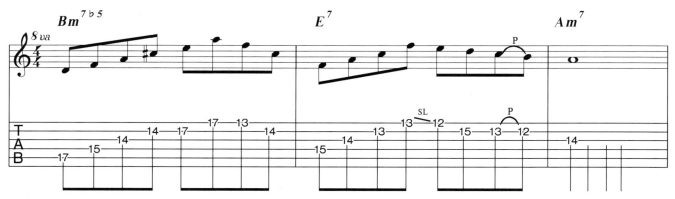

Turnaround licks

The most difficult part of the entire form is the turnaround. Here are 5 more licks:

Lick 1

Arpeggios!!

A^7 : A^7 arp

$F\#^7$: $F\#^7$ arp

B^7 : B^7 arp

E^7 : E^7 arp

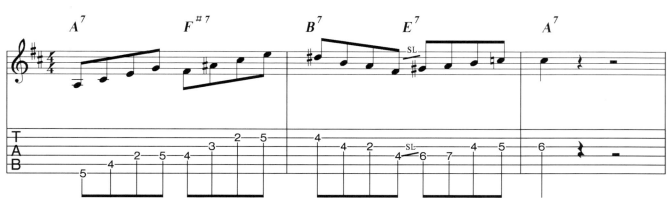

Licks 2 + 3

These two licks are more scale oriented.

A^7	:	A-mixo
$F\#^7$	:	B-harmonic minor
B^7	:	E-harmonic minor
E^7	:	A-harmonic minor

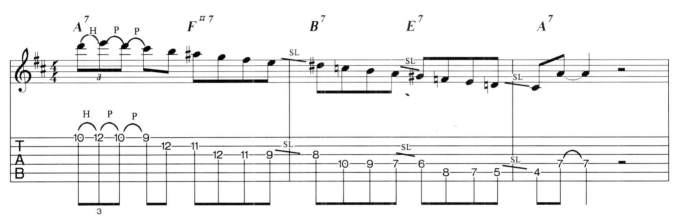

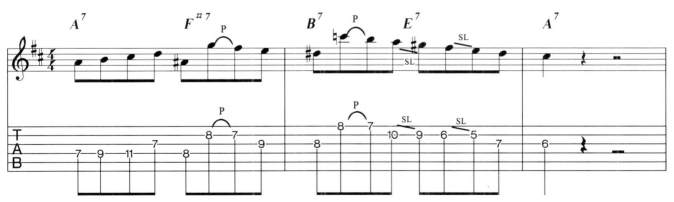

Lick 4

Here triads come into the picture.

A^7	:	A and G major triads
$F\sharp^7$	:	F$\sharp$ and E$\flat$ major triads
B^7	:	D major triad, C diminished scale
E^7	:	F diminished scale

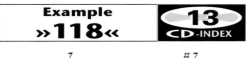

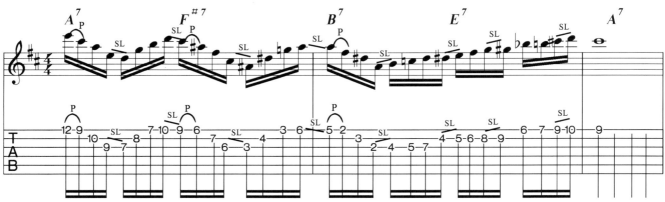

Lick 5

This lick sounds very "bebop"-ish on account of the chromatic notes.

A^7	:	A-mixo
$F\sharp^7$	:	B-harmonic minor
B^7	:	B^9 arp with chromatics
E^7	:	A-melodic minor with chromatics

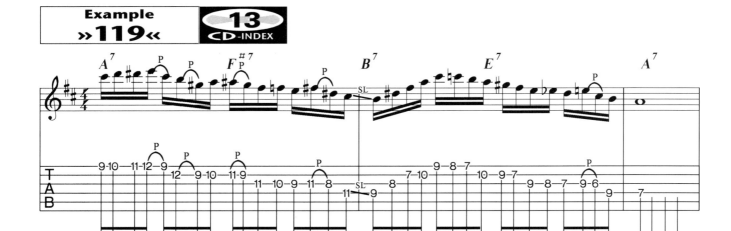

The bebop scale

In much improvisation, particularly in bebop á la Pat Martino and George Benson, not only is the flat 7th used, over the dominant seventh chord, but the major 7th as well. Although this is theoretically the "wrongest" note that could possibly be played over this chord, as a chromatic passing note it sounds pretty hip. Curiously enough, it seems to intensify the effect of the flat 7th considerably. Here are four fingering positions for this scale. Beside these fingering positions you can take every fingering for the mixolydian and simply add the major 7th.

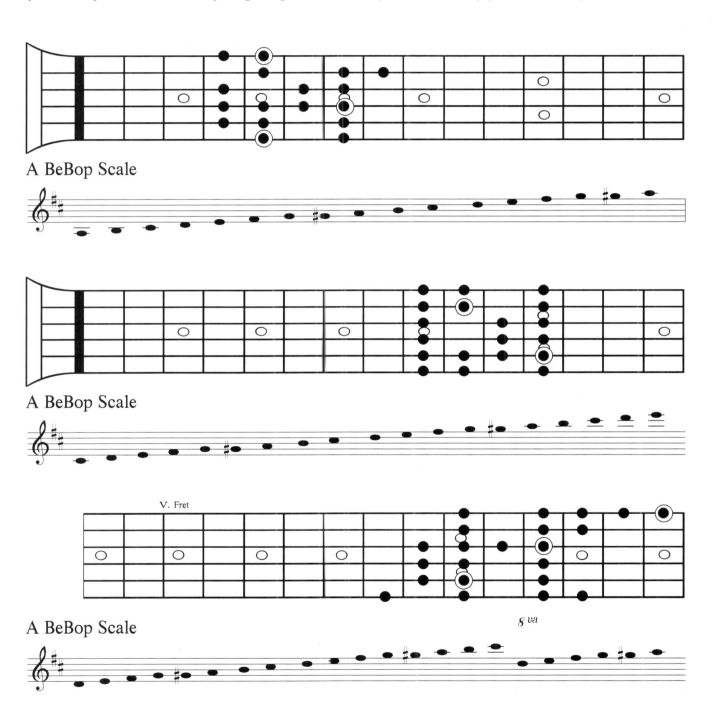

A BeBop Scale

A BeBop Scale

A BeBop Scale

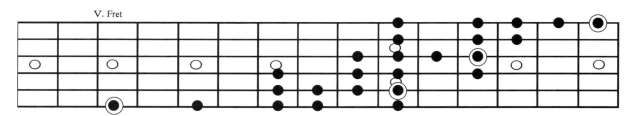

A BeBop Scale

Here are some example licks with the bebop scale. Experiment using this scale over all the chords from A mixo (D major).

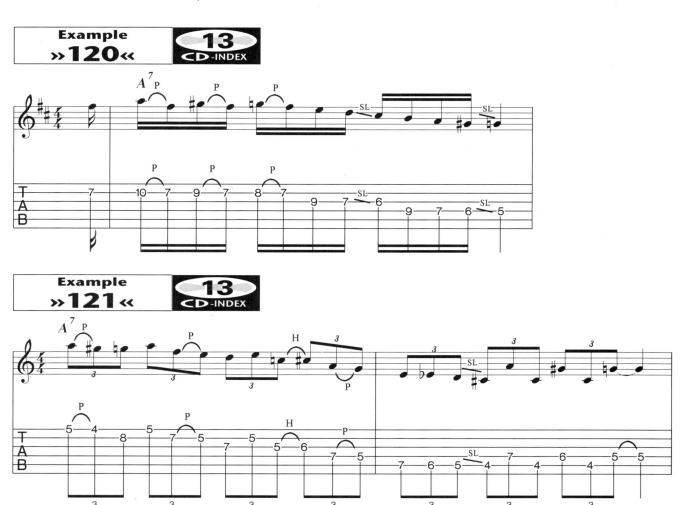

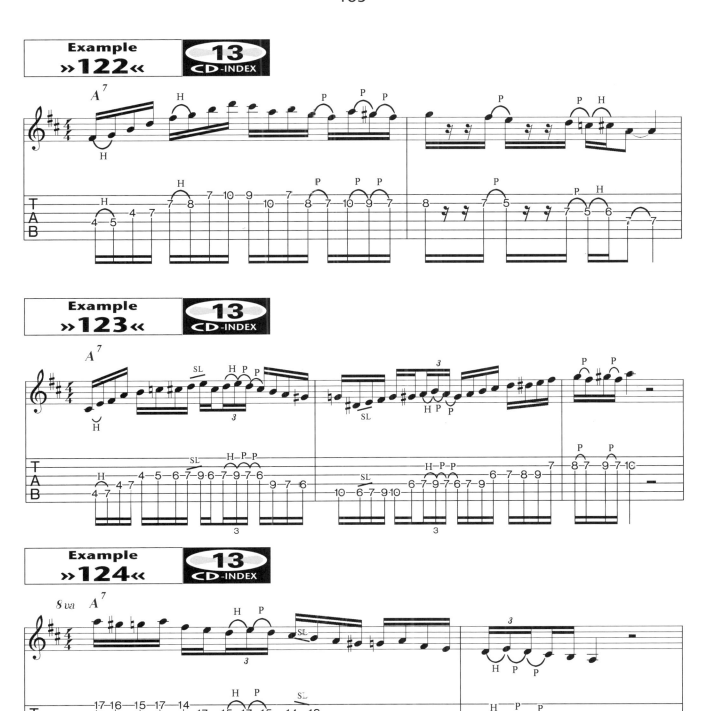

Project:

Hey ... what about doing some scale exercises with this new scale?

Using these licks like building blocks, you should be able, now, to put together endless jazz blues solos. Here is an example of how they might sound.

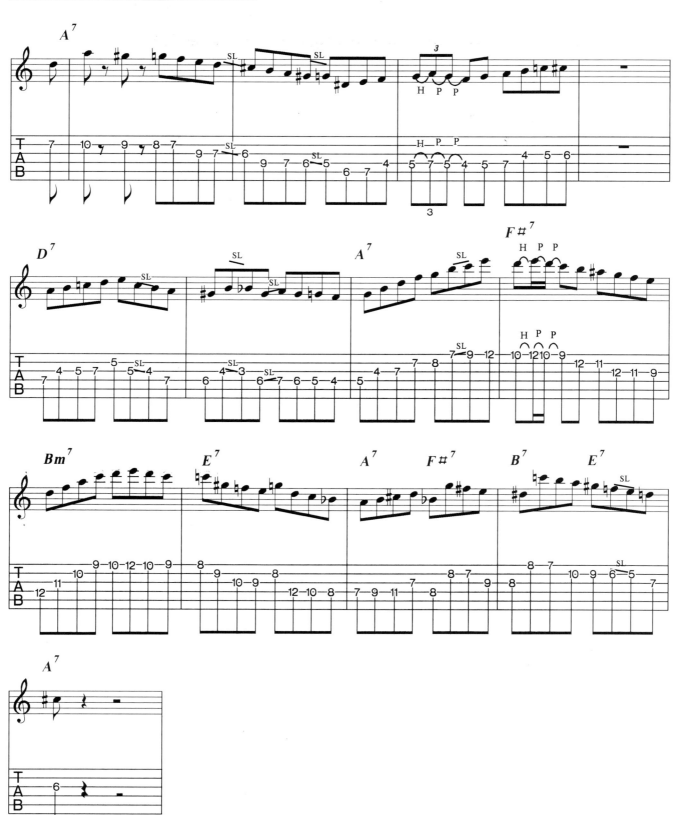

Chapter 17
Classic Blues Sounds

In addition to real blues licks a real blues sound is very important. Aside from a few basic things that one has to know about setting and adjusting the equipment the most crucial factor in getting one blues sound or the other is the equipment itself. With a semi-acoustic guitar like a 335 and a Fender amp you can adjust the knobs till your fingers bleed and play til you drop, but you'll never get a Jimi Hendrix sound. To get the authentic blues sounds beside lots of practice in order to get the tone and phrasing down, having the right equipment combinations is extremely important. Before going into the classic combinations of blues and rock here are a few basic items:

I. String Action
I, myself, am a fan of extremely low action. The prerequiste for easy action is a very flat fingerboard, ie. the curvature of the fingerboard has to be very slight. This is usually the case with modern solid-body rock guitars and Gibson-style guitars. This is not the case with old or vintage-reissue strats. Beside having low action, it is very important that the neck is pretty straight and that the frets are "on" in terms of intonation, ie. evenly spaced. Easy action, of course, makes for easy and comfortable playing, but it has one basic disadvantage: the tone is not as lively and also makes for somewhat less volume. For this reason most blues guitarists have relatively high action. This means having to sweat more by fretting and picking, but the difference in sound is pretty noticeable. Fancy legato licks with this type of set up are much harder to execute, but somehow having to work for your notes gives a better final result. Everyone has to find his/her own compromise between easy playability and good tone.

2. String Gauge
A tender-fingered player like myself usually plays a 009 set of strings. As many of the great blues guitarists have big, powerful hands they often play with appropriately heavy strings. A 010 or 011 gauge is standard. Stevie Ray Vaughan even played with a set from 016 to 058!! For normal hands such a set would be unplayable. Heavy strings and high action simply sound better. Here is a trick to make this hard combination a bit easier to handle: try tuning the entire guitar a half or even a whole step down. This is done by many guitarists, for example: Hendrix, van Halen, Malmsteen Stevie Ray Vaughan and many others. The effect is powerful: the guitars (particularly the Strats) sound much better and are, of course, much easier to play.

3. Pick Ups
To get a rock sound with lots of gain, it is a good idea to set your pickups relatively high. It often happens, however, that the magnets are set so close to the strings that the strings are unable to vibrate freely. For blues, I'd recommend a relatively low pickup adjustment.

Now let's move on to the classic guitar/amp combinations for the authentic blues sounds. Here I'll be discussing the "established" models of guitar combined with the "established" amps.

You can hear the following sounds as well on the solos for the different styles.

A. Stratocaster type sounds – Hendrix, SRV, Cray

Let's start with the stratocaster. This classic electric guitar has been used by many blues guitarists. Three good examples of classic, but differing strat sounds are Jimi Hendrix, Stevie Ray Vaughan and Robert Cray.

Combination 1: Strat and Marshall amp.
This is the starting point for getting Hendrix's guitar sounds. The most authentic sound comes from a Marshall without a master volume at the famous 5 o'clock setting (all knobs turned up full). To get the full-bodied "Red House" sound, play with the neck pick up. Other guitarists who play with a similar combination are Blackmore, Malmsteen, Beck (in combinations with Fender Twins) and Clapton (although he changed his equipment often).

Combination 2: Strat and Fender Bassman.
The basic component of the Stevie Ray Vaughan sound was his old Strat and two old Fender 4x10 Bassman amps, turned up pretty high. To get more gain he ran through a number of old tube screamers before going into the amps, each adjusted differently. As an old outfit like Stevie Ray Vaughan had is these days almost unaffordable, you'll probably have to go for cheaper alternatives or reissues of this equipment. And remember: at least 011 strings and tune down to Eb or D. Also experiment with the different pickup combinations, as Stevie Ray Vaughan switched between pickups frequently while playing.

Combination 3: Strat and Fender Twin (and other models).
Another classic sound is Robert Cray's. He almost always plays very clean and has, in contrast to the round full-bodied sound of Hendrix or Stevie Ray Vaughan, a very sharp biting sound that comes out of the Chicago blues tradition, and almost uses no effects.

Combination 4: "Rock Strat" and high gain amp.
In recent years the basic set up for most strat style guitars has changed in as much as most models are now equipped with Humbuckers and Floyd Rose temolo systems. Combined with high gain amps like tuned Marshalls, Soldano, Peavey etc. they produce, through extreme distortion, a very compressed sound with endless sustain.

B. Les Paul and Marshall

The alternative to the classic Hendrix rig has been, since the days of Led Zeppelin, the combinations of a Les Paul and a Marshall amp. Whereas the Strat sound is a bit more "wirey", this mixture produces a broader, warmer and fuller sound. If you compare the sounds of such guitarists as Buddy Guy, Duane Allman and Gary Moore you will notice what completely different sounds can be produced in spite of the same combination of amp and guitar. All three play a Les Paul over a Marshall and still sound totally different from one another.
While Duane Allman's and the early Buddy Guy's sound is more "crunchy" (more overdriven than distorted), Gary Moore has a sound that has considerably more gain. Whereas, to get his

sound, you're better off with an amp with a master volume and lots of gain, you'll get closer to the sound of the other two with an amp without master volume that's turned up full blast to get power amp distortion.

A closely related sound is used, by the way, by Robben Ford. He plays an SG-style guitar from Fender over high-classed amps made by Howard Dumble together with a few choice effects. This sound is similar to the Les Paul, but not quite so fat.

C. Semi-acoustic guitar sounds - B.B. King, Clapton, Carlton

Semi-acoustics like the Gibson 335, etc. are highly favored by the blues guitarists. As with the Strat, various guitarists play this style of guitar over various amps with widely varying results.

Combination 1: Gibson 355 and Fender Twin (and other models).

This is B.B. King's combinations. He plays his "Lucille" over an Fender combo amp turned up pretty loud and with lots of treble. As this style of amp does not tend to distort so easily, the sound sings, but not so extremely compressed, thus allowing for dynamic playing. B.B. never uses effects.

Combination 2: 335 and Marshall amp.

This variant was used by E.C. during his "Cream" years and by blues rocker Alvin Lee "Ten Years After". The semi-acoustic sounds even softer than a Paul, and, combined with a Marshall amp on full volume (there were no master volumes in those days) delivers lots of sustain and a very hip sound. The only problem with this type of guitars is that they feed back easily at high volumes.

Combination 3: 335 and Mesa Boogie.

The west coast fusion music of the 70's was heavily influenced by the guitar sound of Larry Carlton; his effect on Robben Ford's and Lee Ritenour's playing was substantial. This new sound was the combination of a Gibson 335 and a pretty overdriven Boogie. As these amps worked with two serially connected pre-amp tubes, it was suddenly possible to get gain and sustain at low volumes that were, up til then, only attainable at ear-numbing decibel levels.

D. Telecaster Sounds Waters/Collins

The guitar sound of Muddy Waters' Chicago blues was always a very "high frequency" situation. You can get this razor sharp sound with the bridge pick up of a Telecaster played over a Fender combo without any effects. Texas blueser Albert Collins also used a similar rig. You should not expect a lot of sustain from this combination.

The above mentioned sounds lie, as I've indicated, at extreme edges of the spectrum. If you want to have many sounds available to you at the same time, you'll have to find your own compromise. Keep in mind that you'll have to lower your expectations a bit. To get authentic Gary Moore and Muddy Waters sounds out of a single guitar/amp combination just isn't possible. Beside this you shouldn't, as we said at the beginning of this chapter, confuse the terms "sound" and "tone" with each other: your sound will come out of your guitar and amp, your tone will come out of your hands!